CONTEMPORARY SWEDISH DESIGN

CONTEMPORARY SWEDISH DESIGN

A survey in pictures

by Arthur Hald and Sven Erik Skawonius

NORDISK ROTOGRAVYR / STOCKHOLM 1951

Photographs, plates and printing: NORDISK ROTOGRAVYR

Copyright: NORDISK ROTOGRAVYR, Stockholm 1951

Printed i Sweden

The intent of this volume is to give readers abroad and in Sweden a cross-section of contemporary Swedish design as it is expressed in things for the home. It does not, however, include everything—furniture and mass-produced textiles have been omitted intentionally and may be presented in another volume. Practically everything else in the fields of industrial design, the crafts, and the home arts is represented.

The editing follows neither an extremely modern nor traditional line; the authors have attempted to give a diversified picture of what is being done. The examples are the work of living Swedish designers and with few exceptions were designed and executed after 1940 or in full production after that time. To be sure that the individual designers would be represented by as characteristic products as possible, the selection was often made in direct consultation with the designers. In presenting more anonymous, standard articles we have chosen primarily the work of manufacturers who have shown a quality production. In both cases we have followed, by and large, the lines laid down by the Swedish Society of Industrial Design. The objects have been grouped according to function and not according to material. By using the index, however, the reader can find what he is seeking according to the material, as well as a survey of the products of the various designers and companies.

The authors are jointly responsible for the general planning, selection of objects, and layout of pictures and text. The introductory comments were written by Arthur Hald, with the advice of Burnett Anderson in the presentation; the picture section was largely in the charge of Sven Erik Skawonius, and Lennart Sääf was our photographer.

We extend our thanks to all the individuals and institutions who have placed objects at our disposal and to the designers and manufacturers for their willingness to facilitate the reproduction of material. All of it has passed through the photographic studio of Nordisk Rotogravyr and includes at least as much as a major Swedish exhibition.

Arthur Hald   Sven Erik Skawonius

5

Contemporary Swedish Design

This book presents beautiful things from Sweden, everyday wares, decorative pieces, and ornaments of good design. It opens with two pictures which epitomize the philosophy of Swedish design. One shows a collection of modern ceramics, belonging to H. M. King Gustaf VI Adolf. The King, an archeologist by avocation, has gathered his pieces with a connoisseur's eye for the forms and glazes which modern Swedish artists have given to the age-old medium of clay. The other picture shows dinnerware which a bride might choose in a well-stocked shop, quality goods at moderate prices. The Swedish living standard is such that anyone may own them.

What do these pictures say? They say at least two things. Swedish design

6

Stoneware from H. M. King Gustaf VI Adolf's collection.

involves *both* unique objects which are good art in the same sense as good sculpture or painting, *and* beautiful everyday objects available to all. You often find the names of the same artist and manufacturer on an earthenware coffee cup and on a vase in individual stoneware; on table glassware and on a decorative engraved bowl; on printed fabric yardage and on a unique hand-woven rug or drapery.

In Sweden no sharp division is made between handwork and industrial production when it comes to the things with which we surround ourselves and use daily. There is one quality, however, which we seek to implant in all production, whether handmade or machine-made, marmalade jar or necklace. That is good design. This is more than a question of style and taste. It is rather a way of life which we like to call modern and democratic. The double line, which indicates good design and quality both in unique handmade products and in volume-produced necessities, is an expression of the Swedish cultural ideal. Every Swede should be able to create attractive surroundings, using the many available and beautiful objects which suit him and his habits and among which he can be happy and content. Let our democratic concept be your guide when you judge Swedish design, whether you dip into this book for the pleasure of seeing lovely things—some of which you might like to have in your own home—or simply to get an idea of Swedish style and design.

Sweden—a Big Little Country

Throughout the world Swedish design has always been a welcome ambassador for us; so the individual objects portrayed in this book speak for themselves. That our art reflects the national temperament and living conditions may not be apparent to one unacquainted with Sweden and the Swedes. But as an archeologist spells out from potsherds the main lines of an extinct culture and way of life, Swedish design tells of a country and people in a state of steady development.

Sweden could very well have been a frozen wilderness. It is among the northernmost countries of Europe; its upper boundary on a level with northern Alaska and well beyond the Arctic Circle, its southern point reaching no farther south than Labrador. But the warm Gulf Stream follows the west coast of the Scandinavian peninsula and gives the country a temperate climate. Farthest north, in the province of Lappland—a land of mountains, swamps, tundra, and forests—winter lasts seven months and summer two; the midnight sun does not sink below the horizon from the end of May until the middle of July. In Skåne, Scania, the southernmost province and a rich, fertile land, winter lasts only two months and summer four. Lappland's population consists partly of a non-Germanic race—the Lapps—and some Finns, who have migrated there over the centuries. These two are the only foreign elements in the otherwise homogeneous population of Sweden.

The provinces of Lappland and Skåne with differing climate, topography, and people, representing extremes within the country's borders, have one thing in common. A vital handicraft flourishes in each, producing necessities and decorative articles either for household use or sale. The local handicrafts have acquired special characteristics from the people and climate, from their way of life and material resources.

The Lapps are a nomadic folk. They live on reindeer and follow the herd migrations with the changing seasons. Lapp handicraft is concentrated on the utensils and equipment necessary to maintain life. But the Lapps fashion their finest knives with rich ornamentation and make gaudy belts and ornaments for their clothes which on festive occasions glow like the autumn colours of the birch or the bush-covered Lappland mountain slopes below the timber line. To the south, in Skåne, with its great plains and loamy soil, the arts of women flourish, especially weaving and needlework. Here fabrics, rugs, and tapestries have luxuriant decorative fantasy. These exquisite materials are evolved in a fertile province where the housewife processes her own flax and spins her own wool. The handsome, fantastic decoration represents the abundance—the more-than-full measure—of a rich rural culture which does not need to be sparing with the gifts of the earth. Between Lappland and Skåne are twenty-three other provinces with varying characteristics. Sweden is a large country by European standards, in fact the fourth largest; but has a population of only 7 millions.

Sweden is a land of forests, lakes, and mountains. Its natural resources are timber, iron ore, and water power. While Canada is one-third forest, Sweden is more than half, and the cultivated area is only ten per cent of the whole. Sweden has almost 100,000 lakes and rivers, and waterfalls furnish industry with three fourths of its power. The iron ranges are in central and northern Sweden. The Lappland area is considered the third most important mining district in the world and the central ore fields are known for the superb quality of their ores. Stainless steel, used for well-designed cooking utensils and tableware, is thus as much of a national product as precision ball bearings, perhaps the best-known export article.

Sweden is about a thousand miles long, with a coastline almost five times that. Its location between Baltic and North Seas has produced a nation of seafarers. A thousand years ago the Vikings made the Scandinavians the world's most travelled people: Russia's system of rivers all the way to the Black Sea, and also North America were within the radius of action of Viking ships. The craftwork then produced—weapons, ships, ornaments—represents one of the high points in the history of our art, for the Swedish imagination was stimulated by contact with foreign cultures. Today shipping is one of Sweden's important sources of income, the merchant fleet being one of the most modern in the world. A sailboat or motorboat is the dearest possession of many a Swede, who enjoys it for weekends and vacation days along the coasts or skerries. The country has many types of landscape within its long boundaries, from mountain to plain, from inland bay to endless forest, with skerries, rugged and monumental as the granite cliffs of the west coast, or more friendly and

Material and technique—two of the designer's and craftsman's basic sources of inspiration.

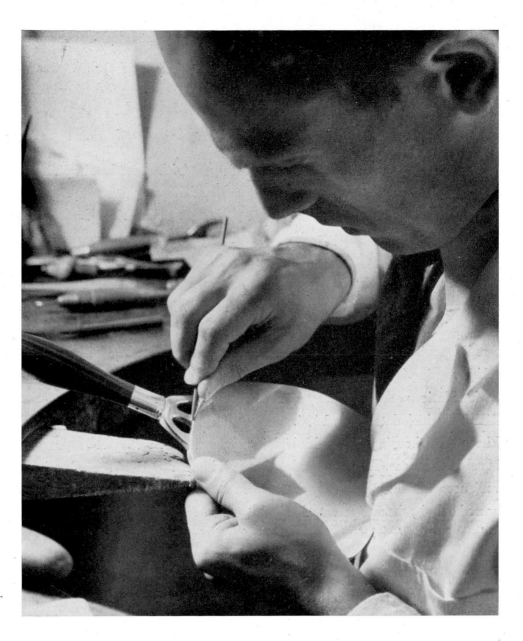

One of handicraft's signs of quality is the loving finish.

luxuriant as in Stockholm's archipelago. In central Sweden these elements of
mountain, forest, water, field, and meadow occur together, a synthesis of
Swedish nature.

Until about thirty years ago, Sweden was principally agricultural. Today the
farm income is still high, but Sweden is also one of the most industrialized
nations in the world. Much of this industry is based on domestic raw materials
—wood and iron; some on imported raw materials. The factories are generally
small—only fifty plants employ more than a thousand workers—and are
decentralized, many being located in the smaller communities, and even in

rural sections. Thus even the factory output offers opportunity for considerable individuality in design and fabrication.

The Swedes in Profile

The Swedes are an unusually homogeneous people. Despite local opinions, there are no chasms between groups, and no very different customs in city and country, or between sections of the nation. An eight-year basic schooling and a living standard which permits travel and study produce similarities in philosophy and way of life. These cut through the variations which stem from political views, position as employer or employee, independent professional man or civil servant, city or country resident. The Swedes are individualists but loyal to the groups of which they are members. The relative stability of Swedish society rests upon a balance between groups. The Swedes have been self-governing for centuries. Sweden is a constitutional monarchy on democratic foundations and is ruled by a cabinet and a parliament of two houses, the Riksdag, which dates from 1435.

The Swedish housing standard is high in regard to technical aspects, rather low in regard to space. Thus the Swede surrounds himself with many modern conveniences, including, in newly-constructed dwellings, a standard kitchen surpassed only by the equipment of a wealthy private homeowner. But the Swede, at least for the time being, lives with his family in space which does not allow the freedom and elbow-room he needs. However, the standard is steadily improving.

But if in winter many Swedes exist in crowded conditions, when the weather permits they compensate for it by "living outdoors." Every summer those who can escape to the country or the archipelago, to live in dwellings which vary from nineteenth-century "castles" of wood with glassed-in verandas to cabins of one room and pantry. Outdoor life—camping, bicycling, sailing, or mountain hiking—provide the freedom of movement and the open space which are regarded as an elixir.

Living "inside" and living "outdoors" are, at least for the city dweller, complementary, and the habits which he acquires during the summer, when he lives simply and directly, are more and more affecting his winter habits indoors. The light, bright atmosphere which is associated with the character of genuine Swedish Modern interiors is something of a reflection from a Swedish summer day. The Swedes worship the sun and verdure, and windows and

Combined kitchen and living-room designed by Gunnar Asplund at the Home Exhibition, Stockholm 1917.

balconies are filled with potted plants which the homemaker tends lovingly and faithfully. Many Swedes dream of someday owning a house where they can "move around" and a plot of ground big enough to grub in because most city dwellers now live in apartments. Modern suburbs are sometimes built up with private homes and villas, however. Sun, light, and air have become a law of life since modern town planning came into its own in the 1930s.

Swedes are well dressed. During leisure hours it is difficult to deduce a profession or position from clothes. Swedish ready-made clothes bear superficial witness to Swedish democracy more clearly than any other branch of industrial production. In fact, if the Swede can be said to live within his income in regard to clothes, this is evidence of both a good standard of living and a good garment industry.

Swedes have a pronounced disposition toward, or let us say weakness for, food. This applies also to the sociable aspects of gathering at the table. Food, we feel, belongs to the good things of life. This interest is reflected in such specialities as the *smörgåsbord*, with pickled herring and other delicacies, crisp bread and aquavit, crayfish, fermented Baltic Sea herring and goose, and in the custom of saying "*skål!*" It is also reflected in the wealth of models and designs for glass, ceramics, and metal which have been created for the

From the Swedish Pavilion at the Paris Exhibition 1925. The "Paris Bowl" by Simon Gate, Orrefors, chairs and table by Carl Malmsten, clock by Carl Hörvik.

Swedish table. This is a field in which not only utility has been the inspiration but where the festive spirit and the joy of camaraderie have brought forth a flood of variations and types. When a Swede has a chance to satisfy both his interest in food and his pleasure in the outdoors at the same time—that is, a chance to eat at an outdoor restaurant in a beautiful setting during the warm season—he is in his glory. Special rites are dedicated to the consumption of the fermented herring of the North or of the goose loved most dearly in Skåne. Eating crayfish is a custom of southern and central Sweden, a ritual whih takes place preferably under the light of the August moon with coloured lanterns in the trees, a brilliant display of fireworks, and a relaxation of manners, as opposed to the formality characteristic of a winter dinner party in the city.

There are strong and ancient traditions which affect the decoration of the table and home at holiday times. The customs of a rural culture blossom into life. Indeed, one of the specialities of Swedish homecrafts has been the making of holiday decorations, in bright textiles, in straw, in wood, and even with foots. But the ordinary meals of ordinary people are more characteristic than holiday celebrations. One of the significant contributions of Swedish artists and

Living-room designed by Sven Markelius in the residential section of the Stockholm Exhibition 1930.

manufacturers has been the creation of beautiful forms for daily use at the table. It is becoming much less common than it was a generation ago to find a double setting of everything, a "good" set of china and an "everyday" set, for example. To be sure, most families have articles which they reserve for special occasions, but on the whole the everyday utensils are the foundation of every service; and these everyday plates, cups, bowls, and goblets which lend pleasure and freshness to any meal are truly beautiful and of high quality.

Swedish Art and Swedish Design

Swedish art, like that of most countries, has had its roots in two places: partly in folk art, partly in the arts of the ruling classes of various historical eras. Sweden was geographically isolated before the advent of modern communications and did not stand among the leading cultural nations. It was on the receiving end, not least in regard to the arts. Not until recent decades, after the achievement of democracy, did Sweden take a ranking international position in the fields of architecture and the applied arts. But because of the previous isolation, folk arts persisted through the centuries, and the foreign styles which did come in developed national characteristics. International styles, succeeding each other through history, have been simplified in Sweden. Her relative poverty in past ages, lack of valuable woods and marbles, and scarcity of precious metals forced her artists to replace lavish materials and decoration with more severe designs and carefully conceived proportions. A good example is seen in the rugged, medieval country churches of granite and limestone with firm, compact proportions, extraordinarily well placed in the landscape; another in the seventeenth-century silver of the Carolinian Era, its severe expressiveness so unlike the idiom of the pompous, international baroque.

During the Gustavian Era, a period named after the Swedish kings Gustav III and Gustav IV Adolf, French influences made themselves felt, and rococo and neo-classic were merged to create a typically Swedish style. The French influence continued into the early nineteenth century when Marshal Bernadotte of France became king as Karl XIV Johan, the progenitor of the present Swedish ruling house. The Gustavian Era set its stamp rigorously on manorial culture and has affected artistic trends even into our own times.

The folk arts, the crafts, nearly always originate as practical applications to household equipment, tools, implements, furnishing fabrics, and the like. These articles are given a decorative design in cases of engagement or wedding presents and for holidays and parties. The popular pictorial arts, painted tapestries, and wall coverings—either permanent or stored in chests for display only on state occasions—were made by popular professionals. Painters in the provinces of Småland and Halland and the better known ones from Dalarna and Hälsingland, modelled their works on the art of the upper classes or used illustrations from the Bible, the hymnal, or religious writings, according to their own naïve and freshly narrative inclinations. The character of modern Swedish design has thus been marked by two influences, that of the folk arts, with their uninhibited decoration and joyous colour and design, and that of the more trained artists, whose severity and simplification characterize Swedish modifications of continental styles.

Modern Design—Child of Industrialism and Democracy

It was, however, neither folk arts nor historical styles which laid the foundation for modern industrial art. It was industrialism itself and a democratic society. When factories took over production, men worked for the first time for an anonymous market. The natural contact between maker and client disappeared. Consumers had the advantage of lower prices but at the expense of design and quality. Ease of manufacture and lack of understanding of the new idiom created by technology resulted in the application of such "refined" historical styles as Neo-Gothic and Neo-Rococo to gas lanterns, iron stoves, and telephones. In England, John Ruskin and William Morris rebelled against the poor quality and tastelessness of industrialism and sought to revive hand-work. Although they won artistic victories, they could not reach the great public with their expensive handmade products. A frontal attack was required, and quantity reconciled with quality through better industrial design.

At the end of the nineteenth century, the *Jugend* or *l'art nouveau* style develops, with its possibilities of escape from the repetitive circle of historic idioms. And at the beginning of the twentieth century the purpose of the German *Werkbund* was the creation of mass-produced articles of good quality and design at a popular price. Such a plan required the assistance of artists who would become members of the team of technicians and workers in the factory. About 1915 Sweden made a similar effort. During the following years the battle cries, *"More Beautiful Everyday Things," "Artists to Industry,"* were shouted by the Swedish Society of Industrial Design, a non-profit organization of which we shall say more shortly. Other idealistic groups, even earlier, sought to collect and preserve treasures of pattern and design from the old household arts, and to promote a vital Swedish homecraft. Such was the beginning of the modern era in Swedish design.

Within a few years a handful of factories and artists succeeded in producing beautiful everyday wares, and also more selective studio pieces. With both categories Sweden made its mark at the "Exposition internationale des arts décoratifs et industriels modernes" in Paris in 1925. An exhibition at the Metropolitan Museum of Art in New York in 1927 followed the initial victory. The Swedish style of the 1920s was described by an English critic as Swedish Grace. Elsewhere in Europe, handicrafts seemed merely to be coated with a decorative veneer. Then *Die neue Sachlichkeit* appeared in Germany. This movement was a revolt against the decorative spirit, an effort to create surroundings for the modern human being based on his actual needs, on the new requirements of machine production, and on the artistic possibilities inherent in each material. In the United States the leading force of this epoch, the Bauhaus School, carried on the program.

Functionalism appeared in Sweden as early as 1930 with an exhibition of industrial art and housing at Stockholm. The 1930 effort to create good surroundings for the modern being still goes on, although the forms of expression have changed substantially through the years.

The craftsman represents one pole in the production forms...

Swedish Design Today

The now often-falsified concept, Swedish Modern, was created during the 1930s. In this decade the international rank of Swedish design was further confirmed through the World Exhibition in Paris in 1937 and the New York World's Fair in 1939. During the 1940s a new generation of artists had grown up while many of the earlier leading people were still creative. It is the production of this period which is presented in this book.

For the most part three factors influence the design of a product—maker, artist, and buyer. Often an exciting triangle drama is enacted by these three, and whether the play has a happy ending depends on how well the final product fulfils its functional, social, and esthetic purposes. In Sweden a central institution, the Swedish Society of Industrial Design, founded in 1845, represents all interested parties—manufacturers (and distributors), artists,

... industrial manufacture the other. A press for punching tableware of stainless steel.

and consumers. The Society, whose influence is considerably strong, has as its aim cooperation with artists, craftsmen, and industry to bring forth good and beautiful things for the public, and thereby improvement of public taste. The Society proceeds on the assumption that the only honourable way to satisfy the buyer's needs is to offer him quality goods. This presumes that the needs of the consumer are known, that the public can be informed and influenced, and that the manufacturer can be prevailed upon to produce practical and handsome things in co-operation with the artists. The whole development of industrial design in Sweden is intimately associated with this society and also with co-operating organizations, particularly among handicrafts.

It has already been pointed out that there is no sharp dividing line between industry and handicraft. Actually Sweden's seven million inhabitants constitute a relatively small market and mass-production of the American type hardly exists. However, what might be called batch production satisfies the important demands of daily life.

The Swedish art and craft industries work principally in small units. Only the ceramics factories, the textile industries, a few furniture makers, and a few glass and metals establishments have as many as 500 employees each and can be counted as middle-sized concerns. Few of these work exclusively with batch production. Most of them also have studios where unique pieces are made under the guidance of the same designers responsible for the standard products. In certain industries like glass, the work is organized industrially but is executed largely by hand. So the border line between the standard and the individual product is variable, and the same working team can alternate between a series of identical pitchers and a specially designed presentation gift. Most of the arts and crafts industries, which appear on the map on page 166, are in southern and central Sweden. Textiles are concentrated in western Sweden, and glass and furniture in the province of Småland. The glass industry is unusually concentrated—about forty of Sweden's fifty factories being located within a thirty-mile radius.

The Manufacturer's Responsibility

What is the manufacturer's contribution to design and quality? Since he is dependent on sales, he must produce what he can sell. Some demand is far from qualified, and to some extent all kinds of products can be sold if

Glass-making is one of the branches which is something between industry and handicraft.

there is advertising. Therefore, the ordinary market in Sweden does not look, shall we say, like a selection for an exhibition abroad. But the important thing is that in the field of industrial art there is a large group of business leaders who are quality-minded and guided by a special responsibility to their customers. They take the position that good design is good business and they place men in executive positions who have a personal interest in quality and

The industrial designer's place is both at the drawing-board, in the factory and in the conference-room.

design—men who consciously follow the program of the Swedish Society of Industrial Design. Their business pays because a growing number of consumers are design-conscious.

Development of Homecrafts

In contrast to volume production there are the handicrafts, one type of which, homecraft, developed from the need of the rural family to produce its own implements, utensils, and ornaments. Today homecrafts are largely concerned with articles to sell, important in districts which cannot support themselves by farming or fishing alone. Since 1912 homecrafts have been inspired and directed by the units (now 40) of the The Swedish Home Craft League. These are administered by men and women who know production techniques, artistic

The real craftsman creates his own product, from the sketch to the final control.

trends and historical development. Through the associations—and particularly through the idealistic work of certain individuals in them—patterns, models, and designs in rural areas have been collected and inventoried. The making of many old articles has been started again, as well as a number of new items. Through field counsellors, the household craftsman, young or old, has been inspired to try new patterns and new projects, and to work again in wood, straw, roots, textiles, copper, brass, iron, and clay.

Swedish homecraft is not one of those culturally valuable but antiquated forms of work. It is a vital productive activity suited to the labour supply and to the skills of rural areas. Indeed, Swedish household arts are a living tradition. A loom is a common fixture in the country home and, where space permits, it is not uncommon in the cities. Anyone who wants to set up a new loom or obtain a pattern for a rug can always get advice from the homecraft associations.

In fact, their patterns and models are now the basis for the homemade fabrics and linen supplies of many families. Because of production methods, skilled workmanship, and qualified leadership, Swedish homecrafts have become synonymous with quality.

Co-operation between artist and assistant should be a mutual giving and taking.

The Designer—Key Man

Because there are so many methods of production the task of the artist-designer varies greatly. As the "artistic leader," he is responsible for the face a factory presents to the world. In the shops he is a teamworker, co-operating with technicians, economists, and others to create things which function well, wear well, and are good to look upon. His duty is to serve and he must subordinate himself to the product's function and the manufacturing limitations. Despite being a team worker he is independent, for he is the artistic conscience, responsible for keeping his intentions from being bungled by haste or routine.

Glass engraving. The artist's intentions can only be realized through the medium of the skilful worker with artistic sensibility.

But as an artist he has a rich field. In his studio he designs and shapes "his" material with no other purpose than to create a "thing of Beauty and a Joy for ever" and thus he has his personal artistic expression. But he also carries on a tradition in Swedish design: the double line, symbolized by the two introductory pictures in this book. The pioneer generation which made the reputation of Swedish industrial art "lived at the factory." The continuity of their work has created a character for industrial art as a whole and their views have been largely adopted by the younger generation.

The Anglo-Saxon type of consulting designer who executes the most varied assignments for individual customers has not yet acquired a prototype in Sweden. There is a trend toward him, although most assignments still lie within the realm of home furnishings. Tools, machines, apparatus, and implements are designed anonymously or by technicians with engineering degrees.

The consulting designer's opposite, the artist-craftsman, who works with a single material and perhaps makes the product himself, is important in Swedish design. Clay, textiles, and precious metals are materials which can be worked without much mechanical equipment. When concerned with these, the craftsman often works directly for a client or a definite circle of customers. He is often in the *avant-garde* of design, while advances in material or technique perhaps more often emanate from the factory studios where there are laboratories and engineers.

A third group of artists works within the field of homecrafts and household arts. Its task is to create new forms and models and to act as an artistic midwife for the craftsmen who, familiar with material and technique, cannot produce independent designs and patterns without stimulation and encouragement.

The skilled worker is also a person not to be undervalued in Swedish design. He is present everywhere—in modelling shops of large industries, in glassworks, at the potter's wheel, and beside the anvil. Through long experience, many have acquired a feeling for material and design which is necessary for following plans and executing the artist's intentions. Sketches and plans! Yes, it is true that the Swedish designer, depending on his purpose, has to make his ideas visual. But much of the most beautiful work to date has come into being without plans, but with the co-operation of glass artist and glass blower, in the silversmith's work with silver and gold, in the potter's shaping of clay, in the weaver's experiments with colours and bindings at the loom. Familiarity and love of "his own" material are characteristic of the Swedish designer. The finest results depend on intimate co-operation of his fellow-workers.

Artistic talent, and a feeling for form and material, are necessary for the creation of beautiful things. But when it comes to useful objects, imagination must be combined with a rational analysis of how a product should perform. Research on function, a new factor in Swedish design, was started during the 1940s as an aid to designing products in which utility was essential. Such an institution as the Home Research Institute analyzes products on the market and makes suggestions for improvement and for new items. Then it is up to the designer and manufacturer to apply the findings. But this institution also serves consumers with advice and information as to which articles on the market meet the requirements for utility and quality especially those used in the kitchen.

The Swedish dwelling in its best concept blends into its environment and does not prefer to show the visitor a stately facade. It exists for its inhabitants as a frame for living, fitting easily like a well-tailored suit.

A home in the country or suburbs can have an atmosphere of cosy and friendly freshness which is another aspect of Swedish decoration. Here the impression depends on an absence of strong contrasts, and builds in a soft colour scale a unity of materials and textiles. Gathering around the table gives the plan of the room. The step into the garden is short.

Everything for the Customer

But the consumer—what influence does he, or more often she, have on a product? A primary one, since it is for him or her that it is made. This influence is increased by the smallness of the country. The gap between manufacturer and purchaser is easily spanned and the market relatively homogeneous. Furthermore, interest in the home and its furnishings is so great that consumers make their influence felt almost automatically.

The public taste is improved by exhibitions, magazines and other publications, radio, lectures, study circles, and special courses. Consumer information

A living-room in an urban apartment shows the aspect of Swedish interior decorating which is closest to the continental and Anglo-Saxon ideals. The stress is on comfort and relaxation. Fastidious design of the furniture and a consequent choice of materials and accentuated textures constitute a decorative effect intensified by the contrast between the lively cretonnes and the monochrome rugs.

through these media is one of the main tasks of the Swedish Society of Industrial Design, which publishes two periodicals of its own: *Form* and *Kontur*. The Society also exhibits wares and furnishings through the length and breadth of the land, and its courses are offered everywhere, in cities, towns, and rural areas.

Today the well-informed customer is acquiring a steadily increasing influence on production. He is creating the balance in the manufacturer-designer-customer triangle which is necessary before a country can produce not only individual things of beauty, but a design-culture which will affect the whole people. Such a culture recognizes no national boundaries; its language is universal.

Our time demands new solutions of dwelling plans. When the housewife runs the house and does the cooking and the other members of the family help her to serve the food, the work becomes easier if there is good communication between the different parts of the house. Here the connecting link between kitchen and dining-room consists of cupboards to be reached from both sides. In spite of the modern approach the interior is based on what can be called a "Swedish style."

Museums are treasure houses. It would be unfortunate if all the world's finest paintings and sculptures were in private collections and not accessible to everyone. However, museums have one bad feature. They foster the notion that beauty is only to be found in them, in their galleries of paintings and sculptures, that beauty belongs only in a frame or show-case. Actually it should be found everywhere, in a book as well as in a painting, in a chair as well as in a piece of abstract sculpture, in a home as well as in a museum.

It would not be possible to live surrounded entirely by masterpieces, expressions of strong artistic temperaments. There are other forms of beauty of a less obtrusive nature—articles with which we come into more direct contact: the book or magazine we read, the chair and lamp of a comfortable room, the rug on which we step, our children's playthings and sports equipment. These may not be signed works of art even though a skilled designer has had a hand in their creation. Actually they should not be works of art but should have some of the common touch and anonymity which gives full play to an object's design, material, and function. We should not always observe them; it would be tiresome to be acutely aware of the things around us all the time. We may do so now and again when we see them under new lighting or when they are moved from one place to another. The reason we have them, after all, is that we have use for them. It is in the using that we enjoy them, not only because they fulfil their function well but because they have something which we like to call good design, implying that they are both functional and appealing to the eye.

We also value things for the material from which they are made and the way in which the designer has utilized it, employing design and finish to bring out the individual quality. Most people do not like to sit in a metal chair: it is hot in warm weather and ice cold in cold weather. But who has not found it pleasant to place a hand on the gently curved arm of an easy chair, where grain of wood and warm tone of finish appeal to the eye at the same time that the hand rests comfortably upon the form? Or consider a book with a fine leather binding or a magazine printed on beautiful paper. Much of the beauty, or we might say the comfort, in the things around us lies in our consciously or unconsciously experiencing the material. We use not only our eyes but in many cases our touch, and to at least the same degree. Indeed the eyes register how things should feel. The senses react positively and pleasantly to everything around us which has been made with reference to the effect of good design and material. Nor is it a question of just *one* material; it is the play of different media, forms, finishes, and colours which makes up the sum of our surroundings. Leather is leather and paper is nothing but paper, to be sure. However, the ways in which materials are chosen and used are characteristic of an era and a country. The popularity of certain materials, finishes, and colours changes constantly. The gold of the eighteenth-century rococo salon has faded away. The modern finishing of wood brings out its own nature more than it conceals it. Stiff brocade has been replaced by the soft textiles of our cosy living rooms. Marble table tops have been replaced by veneered wood; plastic, stainless steel, and synthetic textiles are the materials of our own time. For example, the work of leading Swedish architects and designers during the 1930s was dominated by functionalism. They worked with spare, sober, chilly, sometimes refined effects in combining materials and finishes. Polished metal, glass, and lacquered finishes were Swedish trade-marks in the 1930s. The next decade had a different character—softer, fuller, more sensitive. The illustrations in this book show among other things, the character and tone of the design, colours, and materials in the Swedish home today.

The pictures present individual objects or groups of objects. Together, however, they reveal a greater whole, our surroundings. And this we experience as though in several dimensions in a variety of ways. We take pure esthetic pleasure in a work of art or an ornament, but we look with a practical eye on other things. Anyone who actually looks at the things around him becomes interested in them. Some appeal to our common sense in terms of economy and general suitability, others are associated with memories and feelings. Some are subdued and others scream for attention. The more we know of things the more they give us; the more they enrich our surroundings and thus enrich ourselves.

CHAIRS ash and Cuban mahogany by Axel Larsson, ab Svenska Möbelfabrikerna. TABLE-TOP maple, Firma Karl Mathsson. STANDARD LAMP brass by Josef Frank, Svenskt Tenn ab. RUG by Ann-Mari Forsberg, Märta Måås-Fjetterström ab. VASE engraved crystal by Sven Erik Skawonius, ab Kosta Glasbruk. TEA SET stoneware by Erich and Ingrid Triller, Tobo Stengodsverkstad. ASH-TRAY crystal by Gerda Strömberg, ab Strömbergshyttan. PAPER-KNIFE and BOX silver by Wiwen Nilsson. BOOK-BINDING leather by Elias Svedberg, N. Bernh. Anderssons Bokbinderi ab.

A Corner of
a Living Room

33

For the Magazine Reader

SHELVES FOR PERIODICALS pine, birch and white lacquered metal tubes and CHAIR laminated birch, lambskin cover by Bruno Mathsson, Firma Karl Mathsson. CURTAIN printed linen and RUG "rya" technique by Elsa Gullberg, ab Elsa Gullberg Textilier o. Inredning. URN "chamotte" ware by Edgar Böckman. STANDARD LAMP brass and wood by Bertil Brisborg, ab Nordiska Kompaniet. BOWL stoneware by Karl Harry Stålhane, ab Rörstrands Porslinsfabriker. BIRD stoneware by Tyra Lundgren.

BOOKSHELVES mahogany, metal rods by Karin and Nisse Strinning, Albert Bonniers Förlag ab.
BOOKCASE by Bruno Mathsson, Firma Karl Mathsson. CHAIR birch by Elias Svedberg, ab Nordiska Kompaniet, COVER by Astrid Sampe-Hultberg, NK:s Textilkammare. RUG by Alf Munthe, Föreningen Handarbetets Vänner. STANDARD LAMP brass and leather shaft, silk shade by Hans Bergström, Ateljé Lyktan. WALL-PAPER by Märit Huldt, ab Göteborgs Tapetfabrik. BOOK-BINDINGS (publishers'). PORTABLE RADIO Svenska Radio ab. FLOWER POT Gefle Porslinsfabriks ab.

The Book Corner

Writing place surrounded by books

STORAGE UNITS painted wood and elm by Elias Svedberg, ab Nordiska Kompaniet. TABLE LAMP brass and wood by Bertil Brisborg, ab Nordiska Kompaniet. WORKING CHAIR painted metal, ab Nordiska Kompaniet. POT engraved pewter by Josef Frank, Svenskt Tenn ab. POTTERY by Tom and Grete Möller. WALL-PAPER by Ann-Marie Lagercrantz, ab Durotapet. BOOKBINDINGS on this page and page 31, from the following publishers: Almqvist & Wiksells Boktryckeri ab, Albert Bonniers Förlag ab, Bokförlaget Forum ab, Gebers Förlag ab, Kooperativa Förbundets Bokförlag, Bröderna Lagerström ab, Bokförlaget Natur och Kultur, Nordisk Rotogravyr, ab Nordiska Bokhandeln, ab Rabén & Sjögren Bokförlag, Saxon & Lindström Förlags ab.

Fine Bindings

Top row: leather Sven Erik Skawonius, N. Bernh. Anderssons Bokbinderi ab; Levins Bokbinderi Uppsala Bokband ab; Per Hedlund and Nils Wedel, ab Nils Lindes Hovbokbinderi. Second row: parchment Bertil Kumlien, Esselte ab; blue leather Frostells Bokbinderi; four items paper on board Nils Mörck, ab Nils Lindes Hovbokbinderi; green leather and cloth W. Barkell, Albert Bonniers Förlag ab. Third row: two cloth Håkan Wahlström; cloth Leonard Gustafssons Bokbinderi; three leather Carl-Axel Virin, Esselte ab. Bottom row: leather ab Nordiska Bokhandeln; cloth Leonard Gustafssons Bokbinderi; red leather Charles Sjöblom, Knut Hässlers Bokbinderi ab.

The Writing-desk

BLOTTING-PAD and ACCESSORIES natural coloured cow hide, Joh. Palmgren ab, Hovsadelma-kare. VASE and PAPER-KNIFE silver by Erik Fleming, Atelier Borgila. TABLE LAMP brass, lea-ther, silk shade by Josef Frank, Svenskt Tenn ab. ASH-TRAY by Gerda Strömberg, ab Strömbergs-hyttan.

TABLE LAMP brass and leather by Hans Bergström, Ateljé Lyktan. CASE FOR A PAIR OF SCIS-
SORS and PAPER-KNIFE Joh. Palmgren ab, Hovsadelmakare. SEAL, PAPER-KNIFE, NOTE-PAD
silver by Wiwen Nilsson. SEAL oak and silver by Sigurd Persson.

The Chess board

CHESSMEN faience by Brita Janson-Sweden-borg, ab Gustavsbergs Fabriker, pewter by Marie-Louise Blomberg, Svenskt Tenn ab, co-loured crystal, cut and engraved, designed by Edward Hald, ab Orrefors Glasbruk.

ELIS BERGH: cut crystal decanters and a vase, pipe-bowl and fruit-bowl, ab Kosta Glasbruk.

For the Window sill

POTS by Wilhelm Kåge, ab Gustavsbergs Fabriker. Gunnar Nylund, ab Rörstrands Porslinsfabriker. FABRIC printed linen by Astrid Sampe-Hultberg, NK:s Textilkammare.

Ewald Dahlskog, Bobergs Fajansfabrik ab. Arthur C:søn Percy, Gefle Porslinfabriks ab. Vicke Lindstrand, Upsala-Ekeby ab. FABRIC printed linen by Sven Markelius, NK:s Textilkammare. WINDOWS ab Åtvidabergs Butiksinredningar.

For Cut-Flowers

HAND-PAINTED FAIENCE by Stig Lindberg, ab Gustavsbergs Fabriker. EARTHENWARE by Anna-Lisa Thomson and Vicke Lindstrand, Upsala-Ekeby ab. GLASS by Greta Runeborg-Tell, Ekenäs Bruks ab (top shelf) and Nils Landberg, ab Orrefors Glasbruk. BASKETS Halländska Hemslöjdsföreningen Bindslöjden u p a.

Top left: PORCELAIN and STONEWARE by Arthur C:son Percy, Gefle Porslinsfabriks ab. Top right: STONEWARE by Carl-Harry Stålhane and center: by Gunnar Nylund, both ab Rörstrands Porslinsfabriker. Lower shelves, left: GLASS by Gerda Strömberg, ab Strömbergshyttan, and right: by Josef Frank, PEWTER by Björn Trägårdh, both Svenskt Tenn ab. Bottom, left to right: GLASS by Elis Bergh, ab Kosta Glasbruk and Monica Bratt, ab Reijmyre Glasbruk. "CHAMOTTE" by Edgar Böckman. GLASS by Hugo Gehlin, Gullaskrufs Glasbruks ab. STONEWARE by Trillers, Tobo.

DRESSES by Linner Reinius and Elsa Sjöberg.

Summer

URNS cast iron by Ivar Johnsson and Sigfrid Ericson, ab Näfveqvarns Bruk. FURNITURE painted, bent iron and teak by Hans Bergström, Ateljé Lyktan. URN terra-cotta by Ewald Dahlskog and SCULPTURE faience by Ivar Johnsson, both from Bobergs Fajansfabrik ab.

Designs for woollens

BOHUS KNITTING "rya" and angora yarn designed by Emma Jacobsson and Anna-Lisa Mann-
heimer Lunn.

For Walker and Wayfarer

COMPASS ab Bröderna Kjellström. CAMERA Victor Hasselblad ab, with case from Joh. Palmgren ab, Hovsadelmakare.

LUGGAGE by Mårten Palmgren, Joh. Palmgren ab, Hovsadelmakare. TRAVELLING RUGS in wool. In foreground: Hemslöjdsförbundet för Sverige, in background: Föreningen Handarbetets Vänner, Sätergläntan.

Swedish wood in
Swedish toys

DOLLS-HOUSE ab Nordiska Kompaniet. DOLLS printed cut out material for home-made dolls, ab Nordiska Kompaniet. BUILDING BLOCKS IN SACK and HOUSE, TRAIN, PYRAMID Riktiga Leksaker ab. HORSES Hemslöjdsförbundet för Sverige. RUBBER BALL Helsingborgs Gummifabriks ab.

MINIATURE WEAVING LOOM Riktiga Leksaker ab. ELEPHANT and DONKEY by Gunilla
Holmsten, Svenskt Tenn ab. TRUCK Bröderna Ivarsson. TUG and STEAMER Gemla Leksaksfabrik.
MODEL YACHT ab Nordiska Kompaniet. WALL-PAPER by Josef Frank, Norrköpings Tapetfabrik.
WALL HANGING printed linen by Gocken Jobs.

DOLLS IN PEASANT COSTUMES by Magda Boalt. There are special costumes for children, but nowadays peasant costumes are for churchgoing and festivals; in some provinces not often used. These are from Floda in Dalarna, Karesuando in Lappland, Rättvik in Dalarna, boy and girl from Leksand in Dalarna.

54

The dining-table offers a panorama of Swedish design. For a party or just a weekday breakfast the setting includes many different materials and designs, and numerous methods of production. In the common napery, glass, china, and cutlery, we can see the effects of the slogan "more beautiful everyday things." Freshness and simplicity are everywhere in evidence, and industrial products predominate. An inexpensive set of earthenware is usual with a porous, faint creamwhite body, either undecorated or with a bright pattern or plain stripe under the glaze. On some tables there appears the more expensive porcelain of thin translucent quality with no decoration except perhaps a monogram. Sometimes very large breakfast cups with gay decoration are prominent among inconspicuous plates and bowls.

Tumblers are made of soda glass, the usual material for household ware, since it is inexpensive and strong, although lacking the weight and luster of crystal. Serving bowls and platters are of pressed glass in simple designs, or perhaps of faience-decorated ceramic ware. The cutlery is of stainless steel, a material which has replaced electroplate during the last ten years. It never wears out and never needs polishing. The heatproof earthenware comes to the table directly from the stove, and so is used both for cooking and serving.

The dishes are placed on oilcloth or on a coloured cotton tablecloth. The setting is unpretentious but in each article there is evidence of design. Doubtless because as much care has been taken with the inexpensive products as with more costly ones, perhaps more.

The setting of the festive board may be based on a handwoven linen damask tablecloth or exquisitely worked linen place mats which do not conceal too much of the beautiful teak or mahogany table top. "Living light," the Swedish phrase for candlelight, gleams above candelabra or from candles in low silver or glass candlesticks. The clear crystal of the wine glasses refracts the light or reflects it from the polished surfaces of stem and foot. In glass wine carafes, there is a wide selection of designs since these are favorite objects of the artist-designer, and range from classic diamond-cut decanters to graceful open wine pitchers finished at the forge. The silver cutlery is quite plain, any ornament serving only to highlight material or design. Table decoration is limited to the "living light" and flowers. The distinguishing feature of the party table is exquisite quality.

Among the more expensive articles at the dinner or banquet table are the accessories which are usually handmade: a silver coffee service, a flower bowl of crystal, stoneware, or silver, a cocktail tray, and whisky decanter and glass set, and, of course, the decanter for Swedish *snaps*. The number of designs for the latter satisfy every taste and range from those with amusing animal-shapes to heavy, brilliantly engraved decanters with silver stoppers.

At this point it is appropriate to go for a moment into the kitchen and have a look there at pots and pans and other things. Beautiful may be a pretentious word for these, yet the good material and design of the equipment—pans, mixing bowls, trays, towels and dishcloths of linen, wicker baskets, wooden spoons—add up to something which well deserves such a description.

The extensive research on the Swedish kitchen carried out during the 1940s to make it efficient and pleasant was not limited just to the plan of the room. The design of equipment was also improved considerably. Today the house-wife does not hesitate to show her kitchen, for she is proud of the gleaming stainless steel knives, the new appliances, and even the practical dish-drying rack. Perhaps she shows off her kitchen because good equipment is the "modern thing;" perhaps because she appreciates the one element which the simplest object may have in common with the most expensive—quality.

For holidays—Christmas, Easter, and Lucia Day—the Swedish housewife follows ancient traditions in her decorations. She brings out her gay embroide-ries, her wooden and brass bowls, her candlesticks of wrought iron or carved wood, the straw crowns, the baskets made from roots, and all manner of other things reminiscent of rural Sweden.

MIXER WITH SPOON and JIGGERS silver by Erik Fleming, Atelier Borgila. SHAKER and JIGGERS crystal by Elis Bergh, ab Kosta Glasbruk.

Design for drinking

SHAKER and GLASSES crystal by Edward Hald, ab Orrefors Glasbruk. FLASK silver by Lars Hedeman and traditional aquavit cups, W. A. Bolin, Hovjuvelerare. TRAY teak, ab Nordiska Kompaniet.

Beauty and
utility in
the kitchen

58

BASKET and WOODEN TOOLS Hemslöjdsförbundet för Sverige. KNIVES and KITCHEN TOOLS
Eskilstuna Jernmanufaktur ab, Jernbolaget. BROWN SALTGLAZED STONE VESSELS Höganäs-
Billesholms ab. BOWL and POT earthenware, ab Nittsjö Stenkärlsfabrik. RECTANGULAR BOWLS
oven proof earthenware, Andersson & Johansson ab, Keramisk Verkstad. JARS earthenware by Gunnar Nylund, ab Rörstrands Porslinsfabriker,

PLATE-RACK by Karin and Nisse Strinning, Ingenjörsfirma Elfa. TABLEWARE bone china with traditional decoration, modified by Stig Lindberg, ab Gustavsbergs Fabriker. OVEN PROOF BAKING DISHES Gefle Porslinsfabriks ab. BUTTER COOLER earthenware, Bobergs Fajansfabrik ab. STAINLESS STEEL VESSELS Svenska Stålpressnings ab. BOWL earthenware, Andersson & Johansson ab. BASKETS Hemslöjdsförbundet för Sverige. BUTTER JAR earthenware by Jerk Werkmäster, ab Nittsjö Stenkärlsfabrik. KITCHEN TOOLS stainless steel and plastic, ab Silver & Stål.

Dinner
is served

WINE GLASSES crystal by Elis Bergh, ab Kosta Glasbruk. DINNER SERVICE porcelain by Arthur C:son Percy, ab Karlskrona Porslinsfabrik. CUTLERY electroplate by Just Andersen, Guldsmeds Aktiebolaget i Stockholm, GAB. CANDLESTICKS AND FLOWER BOWL silver by Sven-Arne Gillgren, Guldsmeds Aktiebolaget i Stockholm, GAB. PLACE MATS handwoven linen, handmade lace, Spetsutskottet i Vadstena. CHAIRS mahogany with handwoven linen, ab Nordiska Kompaniet. LAMP AND FOLDING SCREEN by Josef Frank, Svenskt Tenn ab. FOLDING TABLE with teak top and birch trestles, seating a maximum of 12 persons, by Bruno Mathsson, Firma Karl Mathsson.

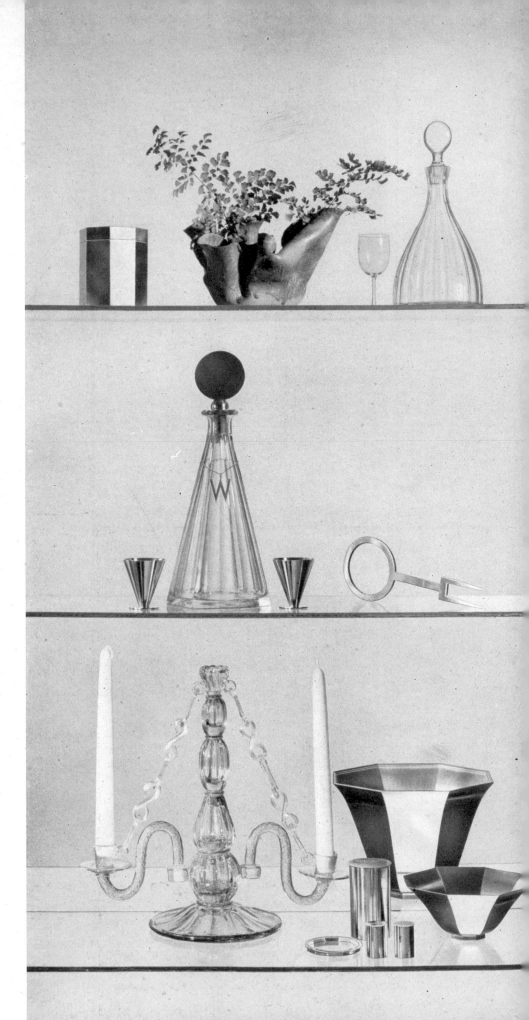

TEA CADDY silver by Wiwen Nilsson. FLOWER POT stoneware by Tyra Lundgren. DECANTER crystal by Gerda Strömberg, ab Strömbergshyttan. BOWL porcelain by Gunnar Nylund, ab Rörstrands Porslinsfabriker. BIRDS stoneware by Tyra Lundgren. DECANTER and BOWL by Elis Bergh, ab Kosta Glasbruk.

DECANTER WITH STOPPER and CUPS silver by Wiwen Nilsson, decanter of crystal, ab Orrefors Glasbruk. MEAT FORK silver by Wiwen Nilsson. DECANTER crystal by Simon Gate, ab Orrefors Glasbruk. BOWL and JARDINIÈRE by Erik Fleming, Atelier Borgila. FLOWER POT earthenware by Arthur C:son Percy, Gefle Porslinsfabriks ab.

CANDLESTICK crystal by Gerda Strömberg, ab Strömbergshyttan. BOWLS and SALT CELLAR silver by Wiwen Nilsson. GLASSES crystal by Simon Gate, ab Orrefors Glasbruk. CANDELABRUM silver by Erik Fleming, Atelier Borgila. FRUIT BOWL crystal by ab Orrefors Glasbruk. ASH TRAY, CIGARETTE CUP crystal, ab Orrefors Glasbruk. WINE JUG crystal by Edward Hald, ab Orrefors Glasbruk. FIGURINE faience by Ursula Printz, ab Gustavsbergs Fabriker. CANDLESTICK crystal by Edvin Öhrström, ab Orrefors Glasbruk.

DINNER SERVICE porcelain by Arthur C:son Percy, ab Karlskrona Porslinsfabrik. WINE GLASSES crystal, by Simon Gate, ab Orrefors Glasbruk. CANDLE-STICK crystal by Edward Hald, ab Orrefors Glasbruk. CUTLERY and SALT CELLAR silver by Erik Fleming, Atelier Borgila. PLACE MAT and NAPKIN linen by Olga Söderström, Nordiska Industri ab.

DINNER SERVICE earthenware by Arthur C:son Percy, Gefle Porslinsfabriks ab. WINE GLASSES crystal by Gerda Strömberg, ab Strömbergshyttan. CUTLERY silver by Jacob Ängman, Guldsmeds Aktiebolaget i Stockholm, GAB. TABLECLOTH linen by Louise Adelborg, Almedahl-Dalsjöfors ab. TABLE LAMP brass by Bertil Brisborg, ab Nordiska Kompaniet.

DINNER SERVICE bone china by Wilhelm Kåge, ab Gustavsbergs Fabriker. WINE GLASSES and JUG crystal by Hugo Gehlin, Gullaskrufs Glasbruks ab. CUTLERY electroplate by Just Andersen, Guldsmeds Aktiebolaget i Stockholm, GAB. PLACE MAT handwoven linen with handmade lace, Spetsutskottet i Vadstena.

DINNER SERVICE earthenware by Gunnar Nylund, ab Rörstrands Porslinsfabriker. WINE GLASSES crystal by Sven Erik Skawonius, ab Kosta Glasbruk. CUTLERY and CRUET SET silver by Wiwen Nilsson. CANDLESTICK pewter with gold leaf by Björn Trägårdh, Svenskt Tenn ab. TABLECLOTH handwoven linen, Föreningen Handarbetets Vänner, Sätergläntan.

The family's table

DINNER SERVICE earthenware by Wilhelm Kåge, ab Gustavsbergs Fabriker. GLASSES by Elis Bergh, ab Kosta Glasbruk. CASSEROLE ovenware, Andersson & Johansson ab, Keramisk Verkstad. BOWL painted faience by Stig Lindberg, ab Gustavsbergs Fabriker. CUTLERY stainless steel and CRUET stainless steel and glass, ab Gense, on teak TRAY ab Nordiska Kompaniet. TABLECLOTH and NAPKINS "cottolin" ware, Föreningen Svensk Hemslöjd upa. CHAIRS painted, by Carl Malmsten, Carl Malmsten ab. LIGHT FITTING ab Arvid Böhlmarks Lampfabrik.

Cutlery
in silver

To the left:
Just Andersen, Guld-
smeds Aktiebolaget
i Stockholm, GAB

To the right:
by Wiwen Nilsson.

To the left:
by Erik Fleming,
Atelier Borgila.

To the right:
by Sigurd Persson.

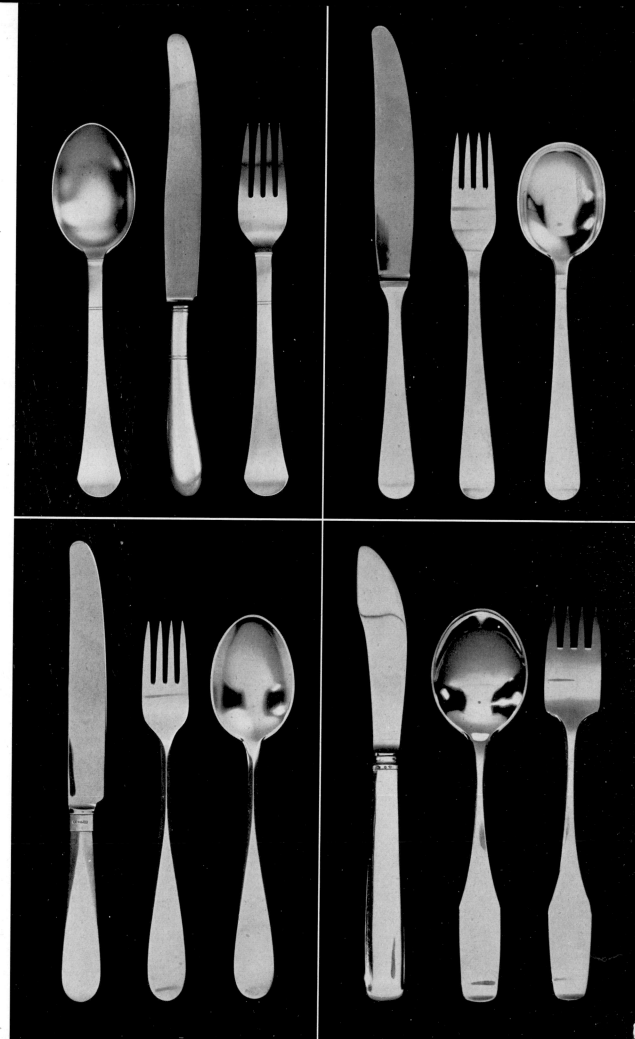

SOUPBOWLS, PLATES, JAR and SALT CELLARS stoneware by Erich and Ingrid Triller, Tobo Stengodsverkstad. WINE GLASSES crystal by Elis Bergh, ab Kosta Glasbruk. DECANTER crystal by Gerda Strömberg, ab Strömbergshyttan. CUTLERY, WINE POT and CUPS silver by Sigurd Persson. FLOWER BOWL crystal by Nils Landberg, ab Orrefors Glasbruk. PLACE MATS handwoven linen by Alice Lund. PENDANT LIGHT FITTING silk and brass by Josef Frank, Svenskt Tenn ab.

A table laid with individual pieces

In the pantry cupboard

WINE GLASSES and DECANTERS crystal by Gerda Strömberg, ab Strömbergshyttan. JAR and JUG glass, ab Åfors Glasbruk. DECANTER coloured glass by Björn Trägårdh, ab Reijmyre Glasbruk.

DINNER WARE porcelain by Arthur C:son Percy, ab Karlskrona Porslinsfabrik.

BOWLS pressed glass, ab Hovmantorps Glasbruk. COLOURED BOWLS AND DISHES by William Stenberg, Gullaskrufs Glasbruks ab. FLASK ab Orrefors Glasbruk.

CAKE-BOXES glass, ab Hovmantorps Glasbruk. DIN-
NER WARE bone china by Wilhelm Kåge, ab Gustavsbergs Fabriker.

COFFEE SET etc. stainless steel by Sigurd Persson,
ab Silver & Stål.

EGG-BASKET Halländska Hemslöjdsföreningen Bindslöjden upa. COFFEE and TEA SET earthenware
by Gunnar Nylund, ab Rörstrands Porslinsfabriker.
TRAYS moulded plywood, ab Bröderna Kjellström.

Cutlery
in stainless steel

Folke Arström, ab Gense.

Folke Arström, ab Gense.

Ab Gense.

Eskilstuna Jernmanufaktur ab.

Plastics: TABLEWARE Hammarby Bakelitindustri ab. DISH-MOP ab Husqvarna Borstfabrik.
MEASURING-SPOONS ab Gustavsbergs Fabriker. JARS Svensk Celluloidindustri ab. REFRIG-
ERATOR BOXES ab Gunnar Fredriksson. EGG-BOX ab Nord-Svea. Aluminium: COOKING VES-
SELS with bakelite handles, designed by Erik Fleming, Skultunaverken. Glass: GROCERY CUP-
BOARD ab Gunnar Fredriksson. Stainless steel: BUCKET Stålkompaniet ab. BAKING DISHES
ab Silver & Stål. JUG Mölntorps verkstäder ab. SHELF plastic-covered metal rods, Elfa.

New functions — new
materials — new designs

DINNER SET earthenware by Wilhelm Kåge, ab Gustavsbergs Fabriker. TABLECLOTH hand-woven linen "dräll", Norra Kalmar Läns Hemslöjdsförening.

CHILDREN'S DINNER SET earthenware by Arthur C:son Percy, Gefle Porslinsfabriks ab. BOWL and JUG earthenware by Ingrid Atterberg, Upsala-Ekeby ab. CUTLERY stainless steel, ab Gense. PLACE MAT handwoven "cottolin" ware, Malmöhus läns Hemslöjdsförening. NAPKIN HOLDER painted wood by Oscar Brandtberg, Svenskt Handarbete. OILCLOTH Mölnlycke Väfveri ab.

TABLEWARE faience by Allan Ebeling, Bobergs Fajansfabrik ab. CUTLERY stainless steel, ab Gense. BOWL turned wood, Föreningen Svensk Hemslöjd upa. TABLECLOTH printed cotton by Louise Adelborg, Almedahl-Dalsjöfors ab.

DINNER SERVICE earthenware by Gunnar Nylund, ab Rörstrands Porslinsfabriker. GLASS Reijmyre Glasbruk ab. CUTLERY stainless steel, ab Gense. TABLECLOTH "cottolin," Föreningen Handarbetets Vänner, Sätergläntan.

TABLEWARE handthrown ovenware, Andersson & Johansson ab, Keramisk Verkstad. JUG and TUMBLER glass, ab Strömbergshyttan. CUTLERY stainless steel, ab Gense. PLACE MAT in bass and "cottolin" by Alice Lund.

TABLEWARE ovenproof from Gefle Porslinsfabriks ab. Brown and green tinted GLASS ab Orrefors Glasbruk, Sandviks Glasbruk. CUTLERY stainless steel, ab Gense. TABLECLOTH linen by Elsa Gullberg, Almedahl-Dalsjöfors ab.

BREAKFAST SET faience and oven-ware. POT Bobergs Fajansfabrik ab. GLASSES Ekenäs Bruks ab. CUT-LERY stainless steel, ab Gense. CLOTH cotton, Halla Textil ab.

TABLEWARE and CRUET SET bone china, ab Gustavsbergs Fabriker. GLASSES crystal, ab Måler-ås Glasbruk, all by Stig Lindberg.

DINNER SERVICE earthenware and ORNAMENT SHELL stoneware by Gunnar Nylund, ab Rörstrands Porslinsfabriker. WINE GLASSES crystal by Edward Hald, decanters by Ingeborg Lundin
and FRUIT DISH ab Orrefors Glasbruk. CUTLERY electroplate by Just Andersen, Guldsmeds
Aktiebolaget i Stockholm, GAB. TABLE LAMPS brass with paper shades by Josef Frank, Svenskt
Tenn ab. TABLECLOTH handwoven solid coloured linen, Föreningen Svensk Hemslöjd upa.

FLASKS from ab Orrefors Glasbruk in handmade LEATHER CASE ab Joh. Palmgren, Hovsadelmakare. CUPS silver in mahogany case by Erik Fleming, Atelier Borgila.

DUMB WAITER mahogany trolley by Carl-Axel Acking, ab Nordiska Kompaniet. DINNER SET by Arthur C:son Percy, Gefle Porslinsfabriks ab. GLASSES ab Orrefors Glasbruk. SERVING DISH electroplate, Guldsmeds Aktiebolaget i Stockholm, GAB. TABLECLOTH Almedahl-Dalsjöfors ab, COWHAIR MAT by Viola Gråsten, NK:s Textilkammare.

Left row: STEW PAN electroplate, Guldsmeds Aktiebolaget i Stockholm, GAB. CUTLERY stainless steel, ab Gense. Second row: GLASS DISH ab Reijmyre Glasbruk. OVENPROOF POTS (blue) Gefle Porslinsfabriks ab. JAR (green) earthenware, ab Nittsjö Stenkärlsfabrik. SERVING DISH (leafshaped) hand-painted faience by Stig Lindberg, ab Gustavsbergs Fabriker. Third row: OVEN-PROOF POTS (white and green) ab Rörstrands Porslinsfabriker. DISH and BUTTERDISHES (leafshaped) handpainted faience by Stig Lindberg, ab Gus-tavsbergs Fabriker. SAUCEDISH (green) earthenware, Andersson & Johansson ab, Keramisk Verkstad. Wooden BOWL and TRAYS Föreningen Svensk Hem-slöjd upa. Upper corner right: DISHES and "COCOTTES" earthenware, An-dersson & Johansson ab, Keramisk Verkstad. Bottom to the right: GLASSES ab Strömbergshyttan. TABLECLOTH handwoven linen, Föreningen Svensk Hemslöjd upa.

For the "smörgåsbord" and the "snaps" (aquavit)

Fishshaped crystal DECANTER by Hugo Gehlin, Gullaskrufs Glasbruks ab. SILVER CUPS by Sigurd Persson.

TEA SET earthenware by Hertha Bengtsson,
ab Rörstrands Porslinsfabriker.

COFFEE SET earthenware by Arthur C:son
Percy, Gefle Porslinsfabriks ab.

TEA SET burnished pewter by Josef Frank,
Svenskt Tenn ab. TEA JAR crystal by Elis
Bergh, ab Kosta Glasbruk. TRAYS moulded
plywood, cellulose varnished or painted, ab Bröderna Kjellström.

TEA SET in earthenware and DOUBLE POT in stoneware by Gunnar Nylund, ab Rörstrands Porslinsfabriker.

COFFEE SET porcelain by Louise Adelborg, ab Rörstrands Porslinsfabriker.

TEA and COFFEE SET matt electroplate by Sven-Arne Gillgren, Guldsmeds Aktiebolaget i Stockholm, GAB.
NAPKINS, DOILIES hand-embroidered linen by Olga Söderström, Nordiska Industri ab.

83

The Saint Lucia Day

On the dark winter morning of 13th December almost every Swedish home commemorates the Italian legend of Saint Lucia. In this traditional foretaste of Christmas a young girl enters, crowned with candles and carrying a tray of coffee and special buns; she is followed by her maids singing a song about the Sicilian virgin.

Here the tray is laid with a COFFEE SET in earthenware by Arthur C:son Percy, Gefle Porslinsfabriks ab and CANDLESTICKS in blue glass by Hugo Gehlin, Gullaskrufs Glasbruks ab.

The central Swedish festival. In the middle of the dark winter it is celebrated with plenty of candles and many traditional ornaments. Red is the dominating colour for Christmas decorations.
Here is a Christmas table with handwrought iron CANDLESTICK, copper PITCHER for mulled wine "glögg"; BOWLS from turned wood and pewter and a STRAW "CROWN," all from Hemslöjds-förbundet för Sverige. The TABLECLOTH embroidered linen is by Ann-Mari Forsberg, Föreningen Handarbetets Vänner.

Christmas

For laying the
dinner table

86

BOWL and SALAD DISHES earthenware by Arthur C:son Percy, Gefle Porslinsfabriks ab. COM-
BINED CANDLESTICK-FLOWERVASE handpainted faience by Stig Lindberg, ab Gustavsbergs
Fabriker. BOWLS, OIL- and VINEGAR FLASKS by Edward Hald, ab Orrefors Glasbruk, SALT CEL-
LARS by Monica Bratt, ab Reijmyre Glasbruk. DISH in electroplate by Just Andersen, Guldsmeds
Aktiebolaget i Stockholm, GAB. Yellow TABLECLOTH silk and linen by Elsa Gullberg, blue
TABLECLOTH linen by Louise Adelborg, both from Almedahl-Dalsjöfors ab.

Hand embroidery

Linen place mats and table cloths.

Olga Söderström, Nordiska Industri ab.

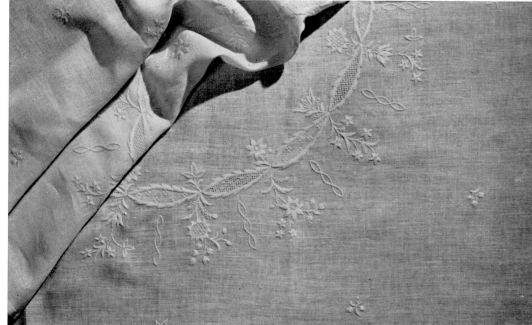

Olga Söderström, Nordiska Industri ab.

Kajsa Melanton,
Hugo Scharfenberg & Co. ab.

DINNER WARE porcelain, ab Rörstrands Porslinsfabriker. Linen TABLECLOTH Almedahl-Dal-sjöfors ab, all designed by Louise Adelborg.

The Swedish Easter table is dressed with traditional decorations—rustic pottery, textiles and feathe-red twigs. VASE stoneware by Arthur C:son Percy, Gefle Porslinsfabriks ab. HENS, ROOSTER straw, Steneby Hemslöjdsförening. BASKET Föreningen Svensk Hemslöjd upa. ROOSTERS WITH CANDLES earthenware by Tom and Grete Möller. PLATE earthenware, Andersson & Johansson ab. Handwoven TABLE MAT linen, Föreningen Handarbetets Vänner. WALL HANGING Grecian linen, embroidered with linen yarn, by Ann-Mari Forsberg, Föreningen Handarbetets Vänner.

Easter

Crayfish party

Crayfish is a great delicacy in Sweden. When the fishing season starts in the beginning of August it is eaten in large quantities, often in the open air under fairy lanterns. This table for a crayfish party is laid on a slate top with accessories from Svenskt Tenn ab. Furniture and textile by Josef Frank.

Textiles are the most cherished and best known of Swedish crafts. Although tradition is strong in this field and the basic technique the same for ages past, textiles first showed the impact of modern design. Those presented in this book, aside from napery, are principally signed creations—embroideries, draperies, wall coverings, and carpets. Such varied types of weaving presuppose a highly developed manual skill and, we may say, a genuine weaving culture in which the loom is not an apparatus for specialists but a living element in many homes. A combination of tradition, personal creativeness, manual skill, and interest in materials laid the foundations for the best fabrics of today. The textiles shown on the following pages have come both from the studios of textile designers and from the looms of those weavers who make no claim to being artists but only give expression to a noble tradition.

The textile designer, working alone, has found inspiration and guidance in a more extensive knowledge of yarn, its production and preparation. And the homecrafts—of which textiles are the backbone—have opened up one of the routes to a general refinement in the quality and utilization of materials. The last decade also brought with it an extension of the function of fabrics. Co-operation among textile designers, architects and builders increased. Hotels, restaurants, and other public buildings offered a broader field of activity which has resulted in greater public interest in furnishing fabrics.

The textile industry in Sweden, as in other countries, has experimented with new, synthetic fibres, but in the weaving arts traditional materials remain the favorites. Modern designs are expressed in weaving techniques with a long, often prehistoric tradition.

The *rya* rug was originally a shaggy quilt. The rya is hand tied, with a long nap produced by knots tied on the threads of the warp. The rows of knots are spaced far apart so that the nap lies flat. If the knots are placed closer together and the nap is shorter, the result is called *flossa,* a technique with oriental traditions. The warp usually consists of linen yarn, the woof of cowhair, and the pile of wool. The *rölakan* was a covering for the backs of chairs and benches before it was utilized in making rugs. It is woven with double, parallel threads of a linen or wool warp and cowhair and wool woof. The surface, unlike the *flossa* and *rya,* is firm, harsh, and serviceable. The Gobelin weave is an international technique with which Swedish textile design produced distinguished results during the last decades.

Lacemaking and embroidery, with their strong traditions, now show interesting examples of the modern interaction between material and pattern. Embroidery or lace, like a drapery or a rug, need not be distinguished from the fine arts, such as sculpture and painting, except in terms of material and technique. Utility is subordinated or non-existent; the brilliance of silk embroidery and the glowing colour in a *rya* make them ornaments for any home.

Tablecloths have become important in the homecraft associations in the last decade. They have a more useful function and more anonymous character than other furnishing fabrics. The tablecloth is, however, bound to material and technique in even greater degree. The coarseness or fineness and the lustre of the linen give the cloth its artistry as much as does the pattern which is bound to the technique—as in damask, for example. These "white" textiles are cherished and, with increasing appreciation of the beauty of wood in a polished table top, place mats and small lace-edged luncheon cloths have received special attention. At the year's festivals tablecloths, runners, wall-hangings and other textile articles, with their traditional colours, contribute to the gay atmosphere.

A wealth of techniques and patterns preserved from the rural crafts survives within the framework of the home crafts which have one character in the province of Skåne and another in Dalarna. The emphasis in this field has been more on the modern than the traditional. Efforts to adapt elements of the design heritage to modern needs and to create something wholly new show that the power of regeneration is still vigorous. This power is also apparent in the fruit-ful interchange between handiwork and machine production.

EDNA MARTIN silk embroidery " L'homme qui court après la fortune et l'homme qui l'attend dans son lit " (The man who chases Fortune and the man who waits for her in his bed. French proverb.)

EIVOR FISHER "Wise and foolish virgins," embroidery on linen in collaboration with Anna Lisa Hellerström.

GRETA SJUNNESON-SANDBERG hand made lace, "Churches," "St. George and the dragon."

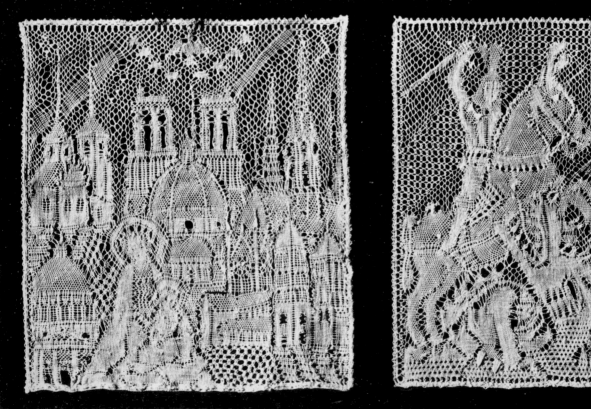

INGEBORG WETTERGREN "A tale", silk, woollen and glass bead embroidery.

Laces and embroideries

HAND MADE LACE from the neighbourhood of Vadstena in Östergötland, the ancient seat of St. Bridget's convent. "Tree of life," Greta Sjunneson-Sandberg, "Polypody" and "Ladder to heaven," Märta Afzelius, Svetsutskottet i Vadstena.

Opposite:

SCARVES silk by Edna Martin. HANDBAG linen and silk by Ann-Mari Forsberg, Föreningen Handarbetets Vänner. DECORATIVE EMBROIDERY "Wise virgins," silk, designed by Greta Mörk, executed by Cissi Guldager. HANDBAG linen and silk by Brita Sköld, Brinkens Vävkammare. HANDBAGS gold thread on silk and on wool by Gurly Hillbom.

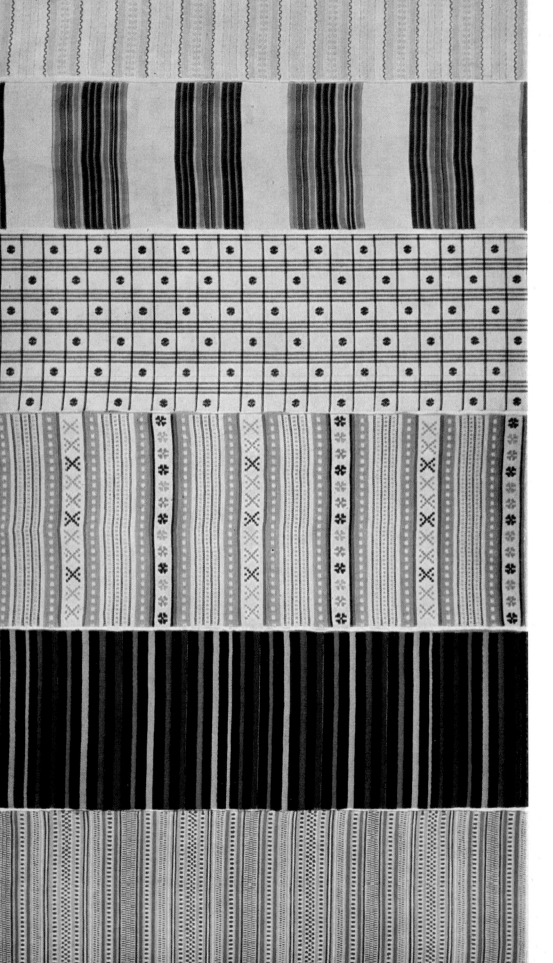

Cottolin, Medelpads hemslöjdsförening.

Linen, Södra Dalarnas hemslöjdsförening.

Cotton, Malmöhus läns hemslöjdsförening.

Wool and linen, Kristianstads läns
hemslöjdsförening.

Wool and linen, Malmöhus läns
hemslöjdsförening.

Wool and linen, Kristianstads läns
hemslöjdsförening.

LINEN TABLECLOTHS as woven
in Swedish peasant homes.

Kronobergs läns hemslöjdsförening.

Malmöhus läns hemslöjdsförening.

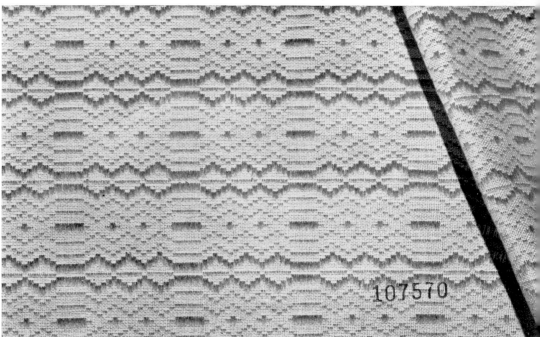

Jönköpings läns hemslöjdsförening.

107570

Souvenirs from a trip
through Sweden

100

Three WOODEN DOLLS in peasant costumes from Värmland, West Sweden, and three from Skåne,
South Sweden. FISHING-BOATS from Bohuslän on the West coast. WOODEN HORSE (unpainted)
from Hälsingland, North East. PAINTED WOODEN HORSES and ROOSTERS from Mora in
Dalarna, Central Sweden. BOAT FOR GOING TO CHURCH as used by the communities round
Lake Siljan in Dalarna by Lisbet Jobs and LilleBror Söderlundh. SCARVES handprinted cotton by
Gocken and Lisbet Jobs, Dalarna. TABLE CLOTH handwoven linen, Värmlands hemslöjd.

NEEDLE-CASE reindeer-horn, Jukkasjärvi, Lappland. SPOON silver alloy and wood, Värmland. BASKET birch roots, Västerbotten, North East. WOVEN BELTS for Lapp costumes, Jokkmokk. DISH Värmland. JUG brass, Uppland, East Central. GLASS BIRDS Gullaskrufs Glasbruks ab, Småland, South West. TABLE DECORATION from wooden shavings, Värmland. COPPER BOTTLE Hälsingland. WOOLLEN SHAWL Småland. Wrought iron CANDLESTICK Skåne. TABLECLOTH handwoven linen. Hemslöjdsförbundet för Sverige and Föreningen Svensk Hemslöjd u p a.

A family of artistic craftsmen from Dalarna

ELISABET WISÉN-JOBS embroidery on linen. GOCKEN JOBS bowls in faience. LISBET JOBS tiles and bowl in faience. GOCKEN and LISBET JOBS handprinted fabrics.

103

WEAVING "Plaice drying" by Ida
Mattsson, De Fyras Bod.
SALT GLAZED STONEWARE by
the brothers Arthur and Stig Andersson, Malmöhus läns hemslöjdsförening.

LINEN DAMASK TABLE MAT
with view from the weavers' window
by the sisters Hulda, Selma and Fri-
da Svensson, Kristianstads läns hemslöjdsförening.

Glass making is a fascinating sight for the onlooker. Its theme melody is heat and movement. The glass—red hot and molten, with a thick sirupy consistency—is shaped on the end of the blower's pipe, which he constantly turns and twirls to keep the glass from running off or becoming deformed. The desired shape is produced by blowing in wooden or metal forms or by free-hand blowing. The molten glass bubble is also worked with primitive but effective tools—scissors and tongs which have not changed appreciably since the time of the birth of Christ. The good reputation of Swedish glass around the world is due to a combination of skilful workers and artists. The glass designer's assignment is different from that of many of his colleagues: he never comes in direct contact with the material while it is being shaped, but is confined to his sketch or pattern of the model and his intimate co-operation with the glassblower.

Art glass is made of crystal, which is heavy, has great refractive powers, and a beautiful ring. The same methods of manufacturing and decorating are used in Sweden as in other European glass factories. For several decades, however, Swedish glass has occupied a leading international position because of the great freedom given to artistic creativeness. The tradition of experimentation has not been broken for a generation. One period has been dominated by thin glass with extensive engraved decoration, another by thick-walled glass in which weight and lustre were most important. The 1940s played the whole register from thin, gracious glass bubble to the massive chunk, both decorated and plain. Affection for coloured glass has been fairly prominent during this period. Such pieces have consisted of uniformly coloured masses in an unusual shade, or differently coloured layers forming patterns in the surrounding clear mass—a development of the well-known technique for cased or overlay glass. By a combination of these techniques, with air bubbles and canals enclosed in glass which give every individual piece constantly shifting aspects of colour, form, and lustre, an abundantly rich variety has been created. Techniques of surface decoration, such as cutting, engraving, and sand blasting, have been applied with an unceasing effort to find variation in expression. Cut patterns have evolved from symmetry into more organic, sculptural effects. Engraved glass was an inportant element in production during recent years but has been pushed somewhat into the background by other techniques or for blown, uncut, and undecorated glass. This does not mean that the possibilities of engraving have been fully explored but that interest in various techniques necessarily undergoes a rhythmic fluctuation. While glass is always glass and retains its basic character in various techniques and designs, clay can give rise to ceramic materials of rather different appearance by using varying compositions and firing temperatures. In addition there are a variety of glazes, which makes the range extensive and rich in colour. The terminology in the field of ceramics varies somewhat in different languages. In the ceramic arts one pole is formed by stoneware which has a dense vitrified body. It is the ceramic material which is fired at the highest temperature—2200 to 2375° F.—and is therefore the most refined. It is glazed, usually with a coloured, dull, or semi-dull coating. Earthenware is the original type of ceramic material, fired at the relatively low temperatures of from 1560 to 1920° F. and has a porous yellow or red body. It is finished with transparent or opaque glazes.

The refined nuance of the glaze and the relation of surface and form are trademarks of distinguished stoneware. It has flourished in Sweden during the last decades in the hands of artists working in the studios of large factories or in their own shops. The glaze is applied to forms of classic simplicity turned by the artist himself or by a capable assistant, or it is permitted to flow into light engraving on bowls and vases which express a modern, personal conception of form. Sometimes a new glaze results from systematic laboratory research; sometimes a new effect comes by chance in the firing which is an irrational factor even in the most modern electric ovens. Stoneware is produced almost exclusively as unique objects or sets, varying a certain design theme. Despite its artistic quality, Swedish stoneware is relatively inexpensive and the hobby of collecting is not reserved to the wealthy. Today porcelain, bone china, and flintware are seldom used in Sweden for decorative objects. These ceramic materials are reserved for dining services.

If stoneware is refined, earthenware can be called rustic. But earthenware can have charming form and character in the hands of one who really understands the material: an old potter, for example, working in the spirit of rural tradition. Faience—with its fresh painted decoration on the creamy white surface—experienced a renaissance during the 1940s.

BARBRO NILSSON
tapestry for a session
room of Hovrätten för
västra Sverige (Circuit
court of appeal for West
Sweden), Göteborg.

BARBRO NILSSON "Vingåkra," wall-hanging. ROBERT NILSSON "Return of the sailor," carved panel in ivory wood, Firma Åhlstedt & Thunholm. JOHN ANDERSSON stoneware, Andersson & Johansson ab, Keramisk Verkstad.

EWALD DAHLSKOG inlaid panel for the Concert House in Göteborg, executed by découpeur Manne Manning, and faience from Bobergs Fajansfabriks ab.

MARIANNE RICHTER "Motley birds," weaving executed at Märta Määs-Fjetterström ab, and earthenware figurines.

EDGAR BÖCKMAN stoneware and decorative relief in chamotte ware.

NILS WEDEL decorative batik painting, executed by Alice Wedel.

WILHELM KÅGE stoneware "Farsta," ab Gustavsbergs Fabriker.

VIOLA GRÄSTEN "Red-lead," rug in "rya" technique, executed at NK:s Textilkammare.

INGRID and ERICH TRILLER stoneware. ALICE LUND wallhanging in cowhair.

CARL MALMSTEN "The dark carpenter," inlaid cabinet front.

STIG BLOMBERG "The Banquet," chased and gilt copper relief executed by Ragnar Myrsmeden. TYRA LUNDGREN stoneware bird figures. INGRID and ERICH TRILLER stoneware.

STIG LINDBERG stoneware, ab Gustavsbergs Fabriker.

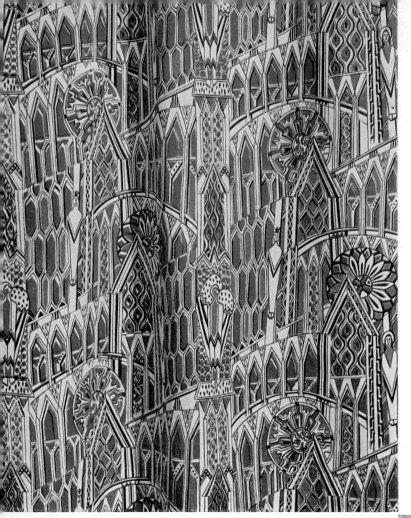

SOFIA WIDÉN "Cathedrals," handprinted linen, executed at ab Licium.

ALF MUNTHE hanging, embroidered in woollen yarn on linen etamine, executed by Föreningen Handarbetets Vänner.

TYRA LUNDGREN relief in chamotte ware, partly glazed, executed at ab Gustavsbergs Fabriker.

ERIK FLEMING Atelier Borgila, silver cup to the City of Paris in occasion of its second millenium from the City of Stockholm.

EDWARD HALD ab Orrefors Glasbruk, crystal presentation to the Go-
vernor of the district of Kronoberg
from organizations in the glass trade.

SVEN PALMQVIST "Selena"-glass. EDWARD HALD "Graal"-glass, ab Orrefors Glasbruk.

INGEBORG LUNDIN "Graal"- and engraved glass. NILS LANDBERG glasses with engraved figure and colour, ab Orrefors Glasbruk.

GERDA and EDVARD STRÖMBERG crystal pieces from ab Strömbergshyttan.

WIWEN NILSSON silver coffee set.

SVEN ARNE GILLGREN silver vases and bowls, Guldsmeds Aktiebolaget i Stockholm, GAB.

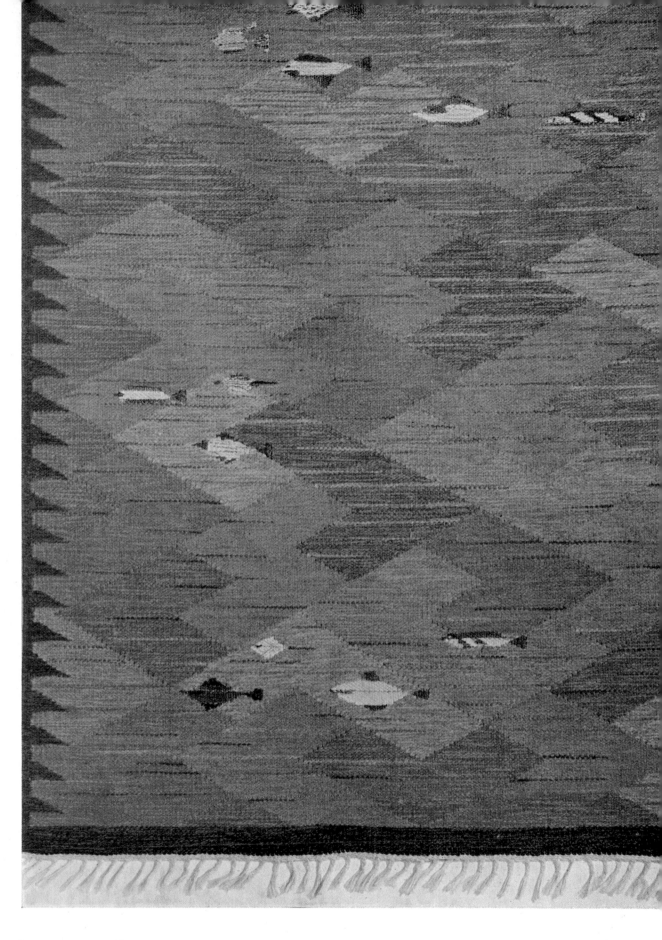

ELSA GULLBERG "Fishes," rug in "rölakan" technique, ab Elsa Gullberg Textilier och Inredning.

PER SKÖLD handbeaten silver objects.

TURE JERKEMAN handbeaten and engraved silver.

CARL-HARRY STÅLHANE stoneware,
ab Rörstrands Porslinsfabriker.

SUSAN GRÖNDAL block-printed tablecloth. LIS HUSBERG bowl in chamotte
ware, ab Rörstrands Porslinsfabriker.

JOSEF FRANK objects in pewter, brass and glass, Svenskt Tenn ab.

EDVIN OLLERS table glass and vase, Ekenäs Bruks ab.

OSCAR BRANDTBERG silver, W. A. Bolin, Hovjuvelerare.

EDVIN ÖHRSTRÖM "Oriental princess," "Ariel"-glass, ab Orrefors Glasbruk.

BERNDT FRIBERG handthrown stoneware, ab Gustavsbergs Fabriker.
ASTRID SAMPE-HULTBERG handwoven curtain, NK:s textilkammare.

ARTHUR C:SON PERCY hand made stoneware, Gefle Porslinsfabriks ab, "Angelica," handprinted linen, ab Elsa Gullberg Textilier o. Inredning.

SIGURD PERSSON silver coffee set and candlesticks.

GUNNAR NYLUND stoneware,
ab Rörstrands Porslinfabriker.

SVEN ERIK SKAWONIUS cut, engraved crystal and etched overlay glass, ab Kosta Glasbruk.

139

TOM and GRETE MÖLLER stoneware.
Wall-paper Carl-Axel Acking and Sven Hes-
selgren, Norrköpings Tapetfabrik.

MONICA BRATT-WIJKANDER glass, ab
Reijmyre Glasbruk. Wall-paper, Ulla Ruth,
ab Durotapet.

BARBRO LITTMARCK silver, W. A. Bolin, Hovjuvelerare.

THORE ELDH silver coffee set, Cesons
Guldvaru ab.

HUGO GEHLIN glass, Gullaskrufs Glasbruks ab. Wall-paper, Elsa Gullberg, ab Durotapet.

JERK WERKMÄSTER tin glazed earthenware, ab Nittsjö Stenkärlsfabrik. Wall-paper, Rolf Engströmer, ab Durotapet.

INGRID ATTERBERG and MARI SIMMULSON earthenware and chamotte ware, Upsala-Ekeby ab.

144

ANNA-LISA THOMSON and VICKE LINDSTRAND earthenware and chamotte ware,
Upsala-Ekeby ab.

ANN-MARI FORS-
BERG "Red crocus,"
wall hanging in "rö-
lakan" technique, exe-
cuted at Märta Määs-
Fjetterström ab.

The Swedish silver of artistic significance comes from a rather small number of makers and studio production predominates. There is also industrial production but inasmuch as silver is regarded as a relatively expensive possession in Sweden and is foreign to mass production, it is handmade pieces which may claim attention here.

There is a silver tradition in Sweden cherished by collectors and scientists. The interest of the collectors is almost exclusively concentrated on past eras, however, and it is easy for the silversmith to be caught in a squeeze between the collector's interest in antiques and the public's strictly limited possibilities for buying and owning silver. Modern Swedish silver is, therefore, based on narrower foundations and has less support from an interested public than any other hand art.

Perhaps it is these difficulties which have led to crystallization of some of the very best qualities of craftsmanship among the silversmiths, a burning interest for their craft, and an effort to bring out the nobility of both the material and the profession. Silver is seldom a product of the drawing board in Sweden, produced by an artisan unknown to the designer. The designer does all the work himself. The individual aspect becomes so prominent that it is undesirable to attempt generalizations in describing contemporary Swedish silver design. During the 1940s a new generation of silversmiths has graduated from the workshops and schools. They have still not acquired profiles as definite as the few silversmiths who led the emergence of modern silver in Sweden, and they show a greater departure from the older generation in their concept of design than is the case between older and younger glass designers, for example. They have one thing in common, however, a love of working with their hands and highly developed sensitivity in treating the dull, bright, or mellow surfaces of silver.

In contrast to the often individual character of the designs of silver ware, jewellery expresses a more international idiom. Inasmuch as the clothes and appearance of the Swedish woman, like her European sisters, are influenced by Paris fashions, the design of Swedish jewellery is influenced by French jewellery. Because of this relationship to fashion, jewellery designing is the most varying of all the handicrafts. When fashions change, many pieces risk losing their appeal. A not unimportant aspect of the work of jewellery designers is orders for the re-designing of "modern" jewellery, where its material value in the form of precious metals or stones make it worth-while. On the other hand, personal affection and material value guarantee a long life for many pieces. Thus the design of jewellery swings like a pendulum between the fashionable and the historic.

The principal function of jewellery is to adorn, but it has an important secondary function as an investment. Economic considerations combined with the desire for artistic value have supported the manufacturing of jewellery at a higher level than that of mere trinkets. Because these pieces are not unique they are reasonable in price, but because the quantity is limited they do not need to be reduced to the commonplace.

A large part of jewellery manufacture and exclusively designed pieces follows international fashions. Among the motifs within the world of fashion, Swedish women have a special affection for the floral. Leaves and flowers in platinum, gold, and silver, with pearls and precious stones, are to be found in rich variation, and their value often lies more in skilful and tasteful execution by hand than in pronounced artistic originality.

However, there is also a more independent trend seeking to free itself from current fashions. A new world of design has sprung up inspired by contemporary trends in painting and sculpture: the abstract and concrete movements, the primitive, exotic art cultures, and Scandinavia's own Viking era. From the viewpoint of material, Swedish makers have attempted to expand the range: glass, ceramics, enamel, gilded pewter, leather, wood, and silver wire have made jewellery into works of design created for their own sake and with an independent life, and therefore usable in more ways than the piece designed for and suited to a single gown or to specific surroundings. From the technical viewpoint perhaps no work is so demanding as the making of jewellery. Minute precision and a painstaking finish are characteristics which here appear more strongly than in any other handicraft.

WIWEN NILSSON silver, rock crystal and onyx jewellery, Hovjuvelerare Wiwen Nilsson ab. ESAIAS THORÉN handprinted silk scarf, Astrid Malmborg Textilier.

148

ESTRID ERICSON, JOSEF FRANK dressing table with accessories and costume jewellery in pewter, Svenskt Tenn ab.

TORUN BÜLOW-HÜBE bracelets and necklaces of rattan, leather and metal wire. CHARLOTTE HAMILTON chamotte ware bowl and GUNNAR NYLUND porcelain vase, ab Rörstrands Porslinsfabriker.

URSULA PRINTZ handpainted faience figurines, ab Gustavsbergs Fabriker.

SIF VON HEIDEMAN necklaces of
dried seeds. SVEN PALMQVIST glass
bowl, ab Orrefors Glasbruk. ARTHUR
C:SON PERCY stoneware, Gefle Porslinsfabriks ab.

EDWARD HALD amulets in "Graal"-
glass. SVEN PALMQVIST overlay glass
bowls. INGEBORG LUNDIN overlay
flower vase, all from ab Orrefors Glasbruk.

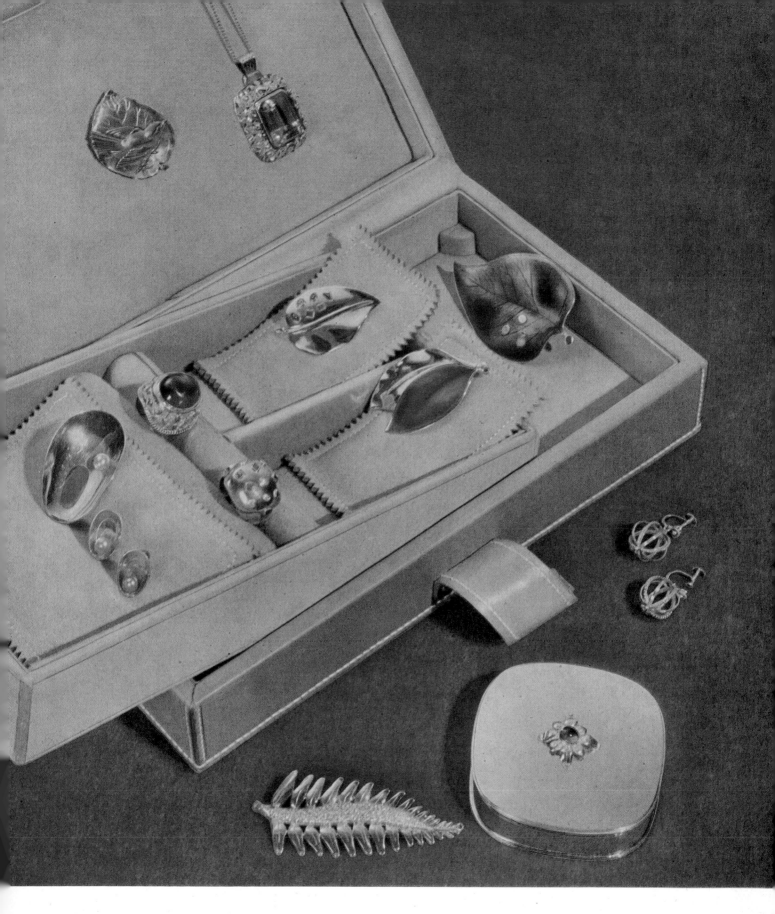

SVEN-ARNE GILLGREN gold brooch, gold pendant with topaz, brooch and earclips in different shades of gold with pearls, gold ring with synthetic ruby och spinells, gold ring with brilliants, rubies, emeralds and sapphires, gold brooch with brilliants and emeralds, brooches in gold and enamel, brooch in gold with brilliants, gold earclips, case in gold and amethyst, Guldvaru ab G. Dahlgren & Co. Jewel case, calf and suede, ab Joh. Palmgren, Hovsadelmakare.

HENRIK BOLIN gold brooches with rubies and brilliants, platinum bracelet with brilliants, platinum brooches with multi-coloured pearls and brilliants. BARBRO LITTMARCK gold and enamel brooch, gold brooch with rosettes, W. A. Bolin, Hovjuvelerare.

BENGT WETTERSJÖ silver brooches and necklaces, Atelier Borgila.

SIGURD PERSSON silver dressing table set, silver and enamel pendant and brooch, gold ring and ring in different coloured gold, silver necklace, bracelet and brooch, gold ring (in case) with green tourmaline.

ÅKE STRÖMDAHL silver vessel, silver necklace and ear-clips with amethysts, gold brooches with baroque pearls and rosettes, platinum ring with emerald and brilliants, gold brooch with brilliants, gold brooch with pearls, gold ring with pale topaz, gold ring with ruby and brilliants, gold brooch and ear-clips, ab Hugo Strömdahl. CASES by Gillbergs Etuifabrik.

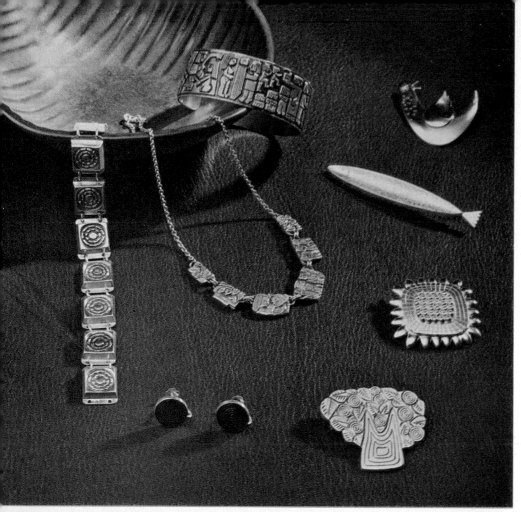

BENGT SÖRLING silver bracelet, necklace and cuff links. PER SKÖLD silver brooches. KARIN BJÖRQUIST earthenware bowl.

HELGE LINDGREN case in gold, silver and jade, white gold cuff links with jade, gold bracelet and necklace with emeralds, knife with gold mounting, ab Hovjuvelerare K. Anderson.

AJNAR AXELSON silver, decorated with
precious stones, Guldsmeds Aktiebolaget i
Stockholm, GAB.

ARNE ERKERS silver, decorated with precious stones and enamel, Guldsmeds Aktiebolaget i Stockholm, GAB.

SIDSEL RÄNGE bracelet in two shades of coloured gold, necklace in gold and silver with rosettes.

TRADITIONAL ORNAMENTS FOR PEASANT COSTUMES tie ring of reindeer horn, Lappland; silver studs, Skåne; silver chain, Värmland; silver brooch, Dalarna; bracelet from bone and silver alloy, Värmland; birch-bark box from Västerbotten and scarf from Uppland, Hemslöjdsförbundet för Sverige.

SVEN CARLMAN silver jewel case, platinum ear-clips with brilliants, sapphires and pearls, platinum ring (in case) with brilliants, gold brooch, gold brooch and ear-clips with brilliants, gold ring with brilliants, gold ring with emerald and rosettes, platinum ring with star sapphire and rosettes, platinum brooch with multi-coloured pearls and brilliants, platinum ring with brilliants, C. F. Carlman Hov-och ordensjuvelerare.

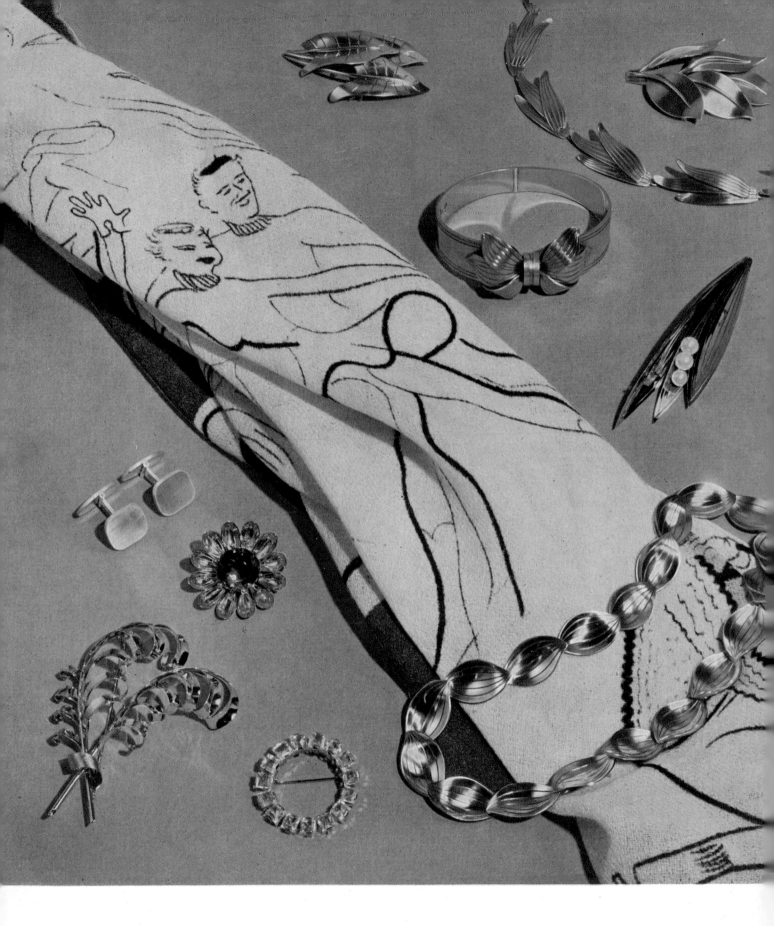

STIG ENGELBERT silver cuff links, brooches in gold, one with amethyst and one with rock crystal.
SIGURD PERSSON silver necklaces, bracelet and brooches, gold brooch with pearls, Ateljé Stigbert. AILI PEKONEN scarf, handprinted wool, Astrid Malmborg Textilier.

162

ESTRID ERICSON pewter and gilt costume jewellery Svenskt Tenn ab. GOCKEN JOBS handprinted
cotton scarf, Jobs.

To the following institutions and persons the publisher and the authors express their gratitude for loans of objects, reproduced in this book

Pictures in the introductory text

Maps of Sweden showing places mentioned in the text

with the older
division into
provinces (landskap).

with the modern
administrative
districts (län).

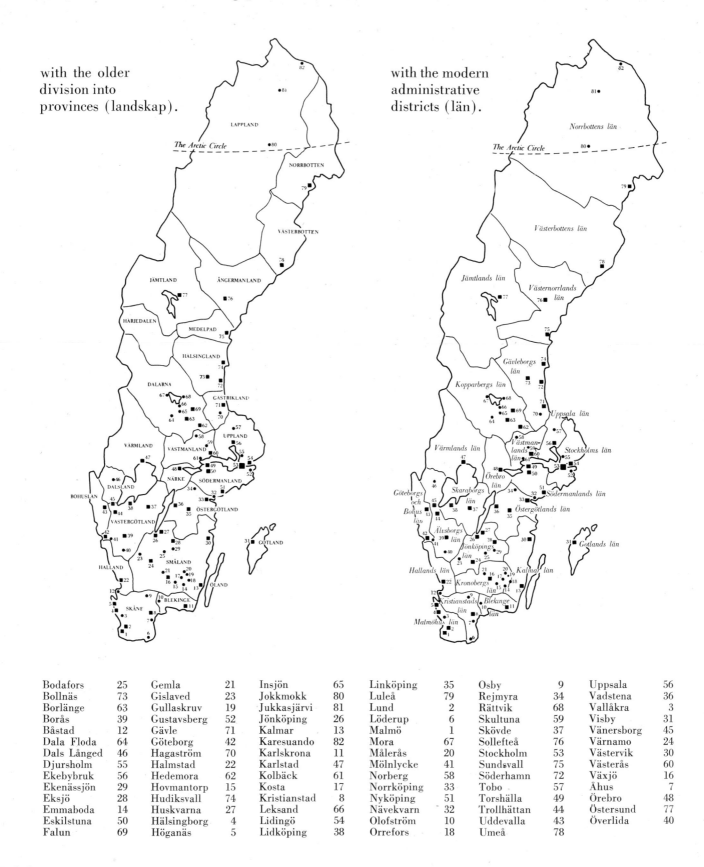

Bodafors	25	Gemla	21	Insjön	65	Linköping	35	Osby	9	Uppsala	56
Bollnäs	73	Gislaved	23	Jokkmokk	80	Luleå	79	Rejmyra	34	Vadstena	36
Borlänge	63	Gullaskruv	19	Jukkasjärvi	81	Lund	2	Rättvik	68	Vallåkra	3
Borås	39	Gustavsberg	52	Jönköping	26	Löderup	6	Skultuna	59	Visby	31
Båstad	12	Gävle	71	Kalmar	13	Malmö	1	Skövde	37	Vänersborg	45
Dala Floda	64	Göteborg	42	Karesuando	82	Mora	67	Sollefteå	76	Värnamo	24
Dals Långed	46	Hagaström	70	Karlskrona	11	Målerås	20	Stockholm	53	Västervik	30
Djursholm	55	Halmstad	22	Karlstad	47	Mölnlycke	41	Sundsvall	75	Västerås	60
Ekebybruk	56	Hedemora	62	Kolbäck	61	Norberg	58	Söderhamn	72	Växjö	16
Ekenässjön	29	Hovmantorp	15	Kosta	17	Norrköping	33	Tobo	57	Åhus	7
Eksjö	28	Hudiksvall	74	Kristianstad	8	Nyköping	51	Torshälla	49	Örebro	48
Emmaboda	14	Huskvarna	27	Leksand	66	Nävekvarn	32	Trollhättan	44	Östersund	77
Eskilstuna	50	Hälsingborg	4	Lidingö	54	Olofström	10	Uddevalla	43	Överlida	40
Falun	69	Höganäs	5	Lidköping	38	Orrefors	18	Umeå	78		

Designers in alphabetical order

Manufacturers in alphabetical order

Manufacturers and Designers according to materials

Jewellery

Metal

Textiles

173

Miscellaneous

Museums and institutions, where Swedish design may be studied and where information can be obtained

NATIONALMUSEUM (THE NATIONAL MUSEUM), STOCKHOLM
Picture gallery containing collections of paintings and sculptures by Swedish and foreign artists. Print Room. Department for arts and crafts etc.

NORDISKA MUSEET (THE NORTHERN MUSEUM), STOCKHOLM
Exhibitions of furniture, household utensils, popular art, garments, textiles, and implements, used in peasant homes and by the gentry in Sweden. Lapp culture.

RÖHSSKA KONSTSLÖJDMUSEET (THE RÖHSS MUSEUM OF ARTS AND CRAFTS), GÖTEBORG

Exhibits of Swedish and foreign artistic crafts and a series of interiors showing the most important alterations of style in recent times. The Museum also displays temporary exhibitions of old and modern artistic crafts in a modern exhibition hall.

MALMÖ MUSEUM (THE MALMÖ MUSEUM), MALMÖ
The Malmö Museum contains collections of arts and crafts from the Renaissance to the present time, archaeological material of Swedish and foreign origin and a collection of paintings.

VÄXJÖ MUSEUM (THE VÄXJÖ MUSEUM), VÄXJÖ
Representative collections of Swedish glass.

SVENSKA SLÖJDFÖRENINGEN (THE SWEDISH SOCIETY OF INDUSTRIAL DESIGN), STOCKHOLM
The aim of the society is the improvement of design in industry and handicraft and the consideration of housing and furnishing problems. The society publishes the magazines FORM and KONTUR.

SVENSKA HEMSLÖJDSFÖRENINGARNAS RIKSFÖRBUND (THE SWEDISH HOME CRAFT LEAGUE), STOCKHOLM
The aim of the league is to promote the Swedish home crafts and their development. It is a central institution and an assemblage of the local hand craft societies in Sweden.

HEMSLÖJDSFÖRBUNDET FÖR SVERIGE (THE SWEDISH HANDCRAFT INDUSTRIES ASSOCIATION), STOCKHOLM
This is a commercial association founded by the Swedish Home Craft League, some associated societies, and private persons. One aim among others is to market, retail and wholesale, high quality hand craft goods manufactured by its members. It consists of the following local societies:

Blekinge läns hemslöjdsförening, Karlskrona
Bollnäs hemslöjdsförening, Bollnäs
Föreningen Bohusslöjd-Konstfliten, Göteborg
Föreningen Hemslöjden, Borås
Föreningen Hälsingeslöjd, Söderhamn
Försäljningsföreningen Älvsborgsslöjd, Trollhättan
Gestriklands hemslöjdsförening, Gävle
Gotlands hemslöjdsförening, Visby
Halländska hemslöjdsföreningen Bindslöjden, Halmstad
Jämtslöjds försäljningsförening, Östersund
Jönköpings läns hemslöjdsförening, Jönköping
Kristianstads läns hemslöjdsförening, Kristianstad
Kronobergs läns hemslöjdsförening, Växjö
Leksands hemslöjdsförening, Leksand
Malmöhus läns hemslöjdsförening, Malmö

Medelpads hemslöjdsförening, Sundsvall
Mora hemslöjdsförening, Mora
Norra Kalmar läns hemslöjdsförening, Västervik
Norrbottens läns hemslöjd, Luleå
Skaraborgs läns hemslöjdsförening, Skövde
Steneby hemslöjdsförening, Dals Långed
Stockholms läns och stads hemslöjdsförening, Stockholm
Södermanlands läns hemslöjdsförening, Nyköping
Södra Kalmar läns hemslöjdsförening, Kalmar
Upsala läns hemslöjdsförening, Uppsala
Värmlands hemslöjd, Karlstad
Västerbottens läns hemslöjdsförening, Umeå
Västmanlands läns hemslöjdsförening, Västerås
Ångermanlands hemslöjdsförening, Sollefteå
Örebro läns slöjdförening, Örebro
Östergötlands läns hemslöjdsförening, Linköping
Övre Hälsinglands hemslöjdsförening, Hudiksvall

Explanation of terms and Swedish denominations used in the text

AB, ab	abbrevation for Aktiebolag, joint-stock company, corporation.
Ariel glass	a glassmaking technique, called after the airy spirit in The Tempest and practiced at Orrefors. Ornaments and figures of coloured glass and air bubbles are put in clear or unicoloured crystal.
Batik	fabrics decorated by the batik technique, which is a resist process. Parts which are not to be dyed are impregnated with wax. The fabric is dipped in colour and then boiled to remove the wax. Repeated as many times as there are colours.
Chamotte ware	a highfired ceramic ware containing granules of fired stoneware (grog).
Cottolin	a textile material where fibers of flax, hemp, etc., are worked to resemble cotton.
Crystal	a fine, clear, heavy, lead glass. Gives strong light refraction. Demi-crystal is a quality between full crystal and sodium glass.
Dalarna	see Dalecarlia.
Dalecarlia	a latinization of Dalarna, the name of a province in the middle of Sweden. (See map on page 166).
Damask	a weaving technique giving a reciprocal effect and a satin surface. Used for different materials; in Sweden mainly for linen.
Découpeur	French word for inlay craftsman.
Dräll	diaper weave, a primitive damask.
Earthenware	a common type of ceramic. It is porous with either white or ivory paste and translucent glaze used for dinnerware; or more rustic with reddish or greyish paste and translucent lead glaze.
Faience	pottery with porous, yellow or reddish paste, covered with an opaque tin glaze, often painted in colours.
Flossa	napped rug, mostly woollen but also linen.
Gothenburg	anglicization of Göteborg, the second largest city of Sweden, on the west coast.
Graal glass	a technique in glassmaking called after the legend of the holy Grail, practiced at Orrefors, similar to the Ariel technique, but used in thinner objects with more exact decoration.
Porcelain	a white, translucent, vitrified pottery with translucent glaze. Used for dinnerware, "vitrified china."
Rya	a type of weaving, earlier used for bed-spreads, nowadays for rugs. It is knotted and has long tufts. Rya yarn is spun from the wool of an indigenous sheep race. The fibre is long, elastic, and strong.
Rölakan	a type of kelim-like tapestry, woven on an ordinary loom.
Salt glaze	is formed by the decomposition of common salt, thrown on the fire grates during the finishing period of stoneware firing.
Scania	latinization of Skåne, the southernmost province of Sweden.
Skåne	see Scania.
Sodium glass	a light, inexpensive type of glass containing sodium; most used quality for daily purposes.
Stoneware	is a type of pottery characterized by a hard, dense, impervious, cream or brown body, covered with different types of glazes.

Contents